Can You Afford to Ignore Me?
How to Manage Gender and Cultural Differences at Work

by Elisabet Rodriguez Dennehy

Library of Congress Cataloging-in-Publication Data

Dennehy, Elisabet Rodriguez.
       Can you afford to ignore me: how to manage gender and cultural
    difference at work / Elisabet Rodriguez Dennehy
       Includes bibliographical references.
       ISBN 978-0615723464

CONTENTS

CONTENTS

INTRODUCTION

"Let us leverage the value of our gender and cultural differences"

Yearning for role models during my years as a young female lawyer, I developed a strong interest in articles and personal stories involving women in the workforce, and particularly their presence in positions of power. Over time I collected quite a library of these materials, ranging from articles in business publications and major research studies to profiles of women who had made a name for themselves.

I had always been puzzled by how often I read or heard about women deciding to leave the corporate world, sometimes after 10 or 20 years of dedication to their organizations. What could cause such an exodus? Why, after all the years of working so hard, would many women *choose* to walk away?

As my own career shifted from law to international business development consulting, answering that question — and addressing gender and cultural issues in general — soon became a central focus of my work. Seeing how critical these issues are to long-term business growth, succession planning, leadership development and global competitiveness, companies have brought me in for leadership consulting, training, seminars, and individual coaching in workplaces in many regions of the world.

To help my clients enhance the role of women and minorities in their organizations, I have found that an important first step is to acknowledge a perception gap that exists. Top leaders in the companies I work for, most of whom are men, sincerely want to help women and minorities achieve their potential, are puzzled why their efforts have not resulted in better outcomes, and express frustration when asking me "what *else* can we do?" There is just as much frustration on the other side when talented employees feel trapped by a "glass ceiling." They too ask, "what *else* can I do? I am well educated, experienced, have worked hard and shown dedication to the organization, yet others are promoted to senior leadership positions while I'm told to be patient."

This perception gap *can* be bridged — with great benefits to the individual and the organization. But it requires everyone to dig deeper into the root causes of the gap — and to embrace, rather than try to erase, the real differences that exist between men and women and between different cultures. In this book, I will share valuable research on these issues along with my own experiences and insights to help you do just that.

* * *

There is a strong business case for organizations to more thoroughly examine, and more effectively address, gender and culture issues. In 2012, the World Economic Forum's annual meeting — attended by 2,600 of the world's top business, government and civil society leaders — made women's leadership and gender gaps one of the key issues addressed in its Congress Hall. As noted there, and in many studies cited by *Harvard Business Review*, Catalyst, McKinsey, *Financial Times*, and other credible sources, women's presence in positions of leadership positively impacts the bottom line.

In one frequently quoted study, "Does Female Representation in Top Management Improve Firm Performance? A Panel Data Investigation", professor David Ross at Columbia University and Cristian Dezso from the University of Maryland analyzed data from 1,500 companies between 1992 and 2006. They found a "strong positive association" between female participation in top management and a firm's market to book value, return on assets and return on equity, and concluded that "greater female representation in senior-management positions leads to — and is not merely a result of — better firm quality and performance."[1]

Industry-leading corporations that have launched initiatives and brought in experts to better understand and develop female talent have reaped significant benefits. Companies are finding that women add different skills and expand perspective in ways that improve strategic decision-making and drive organizational excellence.

To give you a real-life example that supports what Professors Ross and Dezso found in their research, let me tell you about Jane. When Jane began our leadership program, she was an outstanding contributor for a global company, but fairly content to stay in a lower managerial role involving a team of six people. As our training and coaching process developed, she began to realize that she was ready for more and that she had what it took to rise into the company's higher leadership. Her self-talk went from "I should be satisfied with the job *they* think I do well" to "I will think through my path in this organization and learn about business units outside my scope that *I* know I can do well."

This company invested in about six months of our leadership support for Jane. In the three years since then she has earned two promotions and catapulted to the upper tier of the organization. Under her leadership, the company has saved millions of dollars in its manufacturing processes — so there's a bottom line payoff as well as a human one. Consciously planning her *next* move, Jane recently mentioned in an email to me that she had approached her CEO at a dinner event and they had discussed what else she wanted from her career. As she wrote, "it was funny to see the chair empty next to our CEO. It seemed people might be afraid of approaching him, but not me — I saw the opportunity and I took it. I'm ready for more."

Jane's story illustrates what companies can gain by investing in developing female talent. But there are also broader demographic factors to consider. Women are earning a higher number of advanced degrees, making up a larger percentage of the workforce, and rising fast in terms of overall purchasing power. Businesses that don't adapt to these 21st century realities will find it increasingly difficult to remain competitive.

That you have picked up this book suggests that you and others in your organization already know that there is room to improve how you manage women, including those from different ethnic backgrounds, and that you want to do more to advance them through your leadership pipeline. The question is how?

To find effective answers, we must first challenge and refine some assumptions that trap many companies in a cycle of *ineffective* answers. This book was inspired in part by realizing that I needed to refine some of my assumptions too. You see, although I am a woman from a Latino culture, I also had studied in excellent Anglo schools, attended an Ivy League university, and traveled extensively. Professionally, I had many opportunities that honored and developed my unique talents, enabling me to achieve success and feel congruency between who I am and what I do. I assumed, especially during my younger years, that many professional women had a similar experience. But the truth is that, in many instances, women's unique talents, particularly those related to gender and culture differences, are underappreciated and remain underdeveloped in terms of their professional lives.

The experience that galvanized this realization for me occurred years ago during an engagement with a global pharmaceutical company. A group of Latina women approached me during this engagement and asked me to help them deliver a message that they felt was not heard when they tried to express it to management. The message was basically this: "Let us leverage the value of our gender and cultural differences and you will see how much more we can help the company."

Looking at the situation more closely I realized that although executives of this enterprise were intelligent and well-intentioned, they saw gender and ethnic differences as secondary, rather than supplementary, to the corporate culture and their own practices. Their focus was on homogeneity and assimilation, which meant that the unique qualities that would allow these women to add something *new* and enhance corporate performance were not "seen" or were actively discouraged.

My insight here involved overall business performance as well as empathy with the women's frustration. If management couldn't "see" the value of their differences, how could these women envision a path for career advancement? And didn't this also represent a terrible underutilization of a portion of the workforce? The question that popped into my mind that day linked the legitimate concerns of individual women to the business realities of an increasingly competitive global economy:

Can you afford to ignore me?

* * *

Combined with my years of reading and collecting material on women in the workforce, that "Can you afford to ignore me?" moment inspired this book.

As I began developing my initial outline, I realized two things. First, I didn't want to present this as a men vs. women issue. In fact, one "aha!" moment as I began researching the book came from Gloria Steinem's "'Women's Liberation' Aims to Free Men, Too." I read this article as a young adult when it was published in the *Washington Post* in 1970, but 40 years later, I saw even more clearly how visionary it was. One particularly insightful message is that progress requires men and women to have bluntly honest discussions about gender issues and "unlearn" certain pre-conceptions and ways of framing our roles and treating each other. Steinem calls for compassion, respect and a heightened awareness that we are all part of the "bigger story" of humanity.[2]

The same applies to the workplace! When companies and individuals respect gender and cultural differences and see how everyone is part of the organization's "bigger story," both individual and organizational per-formance can reach new heights. That is really the focus of my work and this book. Understanding how gender and cultural differences impact our perceptions and interactions is a necessary step toward creating environ-ments where *everyone* can fully develop and leverage their talents.

With all that said, male readers in particular may feel this book has a "tough" tone at times. But unless our workplace dialogue provokes and challenges old ways of thinking about gender and culture, the complex problems that businesses and managers face will continue. If you feel a little discomfort while reading this book, just remember that you are ulti-mately on your way to becoming more comfortable, confident and effective in managing the diverse 21st century workforce — and that's a win-win for everyone!

The second goal guiding the planning of this book was to provide managers with a more holistic foundation for understanding gender and cultural differences. There is no shortage of studies and books on the history of women in the workplace, workforce diversity, sociological and neurobiological differences between men and women, and many other facets of gender or culture. (Just as there are endless books on manage-ment styles, team building, corporate culture, and so on.) But these specialized perspectives can be misleading if we don't look at the big picture.

In this book, I have tried to assemble the most useful information from a range of perspectives to give you a coherent and more complete understanding. To use a puzzle analogy, I want to give you all the pieces, organized in a way that will make it easier for you to see how they fit together. As with any puzzle, managing a diverse workforce requires the patience and concentration to see both the individual pieces and the "whole" — but as you work on it, the process becomes easier and pieces begin to "fall into place."

To aid that process, the book is organized into four sections. In the first, we'll look at historical misconceptions that still shape the way many of us think, and at key trends involving women and the workforce. In the second, we'll study the real differences that arise from gender and culture. Section III will help you identify gender- and culture-related challenges that may be impacting your company. And the last section offers guidance on overcoming those challenges within the framework of managing teams. Each section ends with reflections, exercises, tips and takeaways on the covered material.

The purpose of the book is not to dictate strict principles that you "must" adopt, but I encourage you to be open to expanding and reframing existing assumptions. Since each section builds on previous information, I recommend reading the book straight through once to understand the big picture, then going back to take a closer look at specific areas. However, understanding that managers are sometimes pressed for time, I will add that if you feel you can only read or assign one section, go straight to Section III — it stands well on its own and will give you much of value.

I hope *Can You Afford to Ignore Me?* will become part of your management library, a reference that will aid you again and again as your questions, interests, and immediate challenges change with time. Just as importantly, I hope you will use the book, and your own insights and experiences after reading it, to enhance a larger dialogue with colleagues and people you manage.

* * *

The title of this book poses a question — but most of us know the answer. In an increasingly global economy where women now make up half of the workforce (more in some industries), companies *cannot* afford to ignore challenges related to gender and cultural differences. The world is shrinking — and we need to embrace the opportunity to put our arms around it.

In my work with corporations and individuals in the global arena, I regularly witness the challenges and frustrations surrounding the issues discussed in this book. Sometimes managers find these challenges over-whelming or impossible to decipher. But I can also assure you, from personal experience, that there *is* a path forward.

Synthesizing a wide range of research, years of my own experiences, and the guiding insights I provide to my consulting clients, this book will help you find that path and bridge the gender and culture gaps that pre-vent promising employees from reaching their full potential. Reframing your approach in order to more effectively develop and promote female and multicultural talent will yield many benefits: attracting and retaining valuable professionals who might otherwise "choose to walk away," achieving more balanced strategic decision-making, improving the pro-ductivity of internal teams, and enhancing many areas of day-to-day business performance.

Welcome to my world! Now let's start our journey.

Elisabet Rodriguez Dennehy, President
Rodriguez & Associates

October 2012

SECTION I — BACKGROUND

Where We Are...and How We Got Here

The 21st century has brought tremendous change to almost every area of business: increased globalization of markets and supply chains, greater competition, diversification of the workforce, broader demand from customers and other stakeholders, and more. Change has become a constant — and the pace of change continues to accelerate.

For executives and managers, the challenges of this rapidly changing environment have made one strategic variable increasingly important: your people.

In every market I regularly consult in — the U.S., Latin America, and Europe — I find senior executives, mostly men, wrestling with similar workforce and leadership development issues. To remain competitive, they know they must attract, retain and develop top talent, improve decision-making processes, strengthen the corporate culture, and continuously improve quality and productivity. They know that a viable succession plan is critical to long-term growth. They understand that all of this depends on keeping employees fully engaged and committed — and that they *can't* ignore the growing percentage of employees who are women. They contact me with a common dilemma: "Our company has talented women. We want to enhance their presence and get them into prominent leadership roles, but we seem to lose them along the way. What else can we do to retain them and help them reach the next level?"

To answer that question, I start with a more fundamental question: What's holding them back? In other words, we have to identify and address the root causes of the problem, or new "solutions" will continue to be ineffective. In my experience, those root causes almost always involve a lack of understanding and appreciation for gender and culture differences.

To understand those differences, we must first learn about their historical and social contexts — and "unlearn" some misconceptions that have plagued men and women alike for decades. So in this section, we'll help you form a more accurate "schema" or framework regarding how we got to our present state. Knowing where we are, and how we got here, is essential to plotting a better path forward.

CHAPTER 1
Three Historical Misconceptions
Holding Us *All* Back

To begin, let's look at three cultural misconceptions that create significant barriers to effective communication and working relationships between men and women:

- Women are the weaker sex; their primary role is to care for others.
- Women are not ambitious; their planning skills are better suited to the home than to career achievement.
- It's acceptable to pay women less than men for the same work.

To one degree or another, I have found these three misconceptions plaguing almost every cultural environment I've encountered. They also came up frequently during my research for the book. One resource I drew upon for this chapter, the Women's International Center website at www.wic.com, includes a list of associations made with women, including that women are the weaker sex. I highly recommend this website if you'd like to explore women's issues further on your own.

The prevalence of the three misconceptions I've listed should not be underestimated just because it has become less acceptable to say them aloud. They are deep in our culture and individual psyches and manifest in many subtle, but very impacting, ways. They affect women as well as men, and in some cases are implicit in organizational processes and practices.

So let's dare to speak the statements aloud, and then dive beneath the surface to understand how such misconceptions may still be obstacles to creating a work environment that will facilitate higher levels of engagement and performance from women.

Misconception 1: Women Are Weaker

Women have long been portrayed as the weaker sex: in need of protection, more physically and psychologically vulnerable, too emotionally sensitive, and not as resilient as men. In most countries, it wasn't long ago that women were virtually (and even legally) owned by their husbands — and that is still a reality in some cultures.

The "weaker sex" myth arises again and again to argue that women shouldn't have certain roles in society. It was why they shouldn't be allowed to vote, why they shouldn't be in positions of political power — and, yes, why they aren't "ready" for the C-suite.

You don't have to do much research, of course, to find that, at every step of our social evolution, women and men have weathered the same hardships, endured similar physical and psychological challenges, and made equal, if sometimes different, contributions to society. They have done this *in addition* to bearing and raising children and almost always handling most household management responsibilities.[3]

It is understandable that some women say, wait, who *is* the weaker sex here?

Unfortunately, disproving or disavowing the "women are weaker" myth in general isn't the end of the problem. The more difficult task is to identify and uproot the myth's enduring influence on how men and women perceive each other and interact.

In my experiences as a consultant, a common variation on the "women are weaker" theme arises when assessing whether a woman should be given a promotion or strategic assignment she has been expecting or requesting. Managers often confide something like this to me: "Mary is very capable and works hard, but she might not have the stamina or strength to perform that job by herself. She seems better suited to supporting upper management or taking a lateral role."

Although it is sometimes true that a specific woman, or man, isn't up to the tasks of a new position or assignment, men and women seldom receive the same treatment in that situation. Men who aren't quite ready typically receive the training and guidance they need to *become* ready, or are allowed to "grow into" a position. Those in charge of development are usually men, adding another layer of support to the process.

16

Women, however, are consistently told to be patient and conform with the status quo. If they're given training or support to prepare them for future opportunities, it tends to be from a traditional male perspective, which isn't always effective. The result is not just that fewer women make it into the company's leadership — this also creates an environment where women stop *trying* to advance, become less engaged, and may walk away from the organization altogether. In this way, the "women are weaker" myth becomes a self-fulfilling prophecy — further reinforcing male misperceptions.

The good news, from my own experience, is that companies can break this cycle by providing women with training and support that matches their needs and complementary abilities *as* women. This is what my firm specializes in — and slowly but surely, this is what more companies are realizing they need.

One senior vice president told me their company wanted a program "to enhance the attributes and skills that make our participants uniquely qualified" and lamented that "I'm not impressed with the traditional training formats that push everyone to be the same and are, frankly, male-driven rather than based on individual considerations." I knew our program would be fully appreciated at that company!

When we start an engagement, there is often doubt among men as to whether our program will work — and a degree of mistrust among women. Most have been through other training programs without much change in their performance or in how senior executives perceive them. When our program gets results, with both men and women becoming more confident and relaxed in their interactions, executives sometimes ask incredulously, "How did you do that?"

It's not magic. Most training, and most business processes in general, are designed to fit men. All we have done is adapt training and coaching to better match the needs and learning styles of professional women. That includes identifying and reframing certain assumptions and behavioral tendencies that may be obstacles to greater success. As we'll see throughout this book, the real "magic" is to see gender and culture differences as strengths to be embraced — individually and organizationally — rather than liabilities to be ignored or suppressed.

Misconception 2:
Women Aren't ("Shouldn't" Be?) Ambitious

I had an "aha!" moment about women and ambition during my first engagement in the Czech Republic. I had been asked by a group of executive women from a major European bank to help launch a women's leadership initiative congruent with the vision articulated by the bank's CEO. In preparation, I interviewed some of the female executives, researched the bank's culture, and familiarized myself with Czech culture by reaching out to friends and peers who had worked there. The profile I developed of my audience was intelligent, driven, committed and ambitious women in a dynamically evolving country. I was very excited to work with them.

I try to be at least an hour early at any venue where I'm doing training, in part to get a "feel" for the group before we start. As I was mingling and meeting people, I overheard the word "ambition" and my attention zoomed in on a discussion involving concerns that attending this event could be perceived by many of the top male managers as women being "too ambitious."

So, before starting the program I had developed, I decided to take a chance and ask an open-ended question: "What comes to mind when you hear the word ambition?"

The response was fascinating. Clearly, ambition was not a comfortable concept, and several participants acknowledged that it was perceived as a male attribute not "fitting" for women. The one exception, a recently hired young woman, raised her hand, stood up and said, "I'm ambitious. I love the word and I think it's important to try on for size." A more senior woman immediately responded with something like, "Wait until you spend some time at work and see what happens."

Since this experience, I have started all my programs this way. The topic of ambition is covered during my training program, but leading off with that question definitely "warms up" the room! Unfortunately, I must say that everywhere I go the response has been similar. For most women, the word "ambition" has a hard resonance. I should add that I also inevitably find a few outliers who "love" the word. Informally, I always leverage their presence as a teaching resource.

The real question we have to ask, of course, is why this misconception that women can't, or shouldn't, be ambitious persists?

One explanation is that having children and caring for the home and family continue to be the primary social roles expected of women in most countries. That has far-reaching impact on men's perceptions in general and narrows the options for women. It also creates a psychological tension. Even very successful women typically acknowledge feeling torn between their desire for education and a career and the internal and external forces telling them that "success" really means raising children and being a good housewife.

Consequently, being "ambitious" in ways that are valued in corporate culture *is* more complex and elusive for women than for men. But it's wrong to conclude that women simply aren't ambitious. In fact, there is one area where the "ambition gap" between men and women has closed or even reversed: education.

Up to the 1950s in the U.S. and most other countries, women received limited exposure and encouragement when it came to education. Family, teachers, and society in general all emphasized that a woman's most significant role was as a homemaker, so there wasn't much incentive or support for young women to pursue higher education, much less think about professional growth and development.

As education became more valued generally throughout the 1960s and 1970s, girls began to achieve more scholastically, including getting better grades than boys. Still, most women didn't pursue higher education, or dropped out to marry before completing degrees, in part because neither families nor teachers encouraged them to prepare for any future other than marriage and motherhood. The social stigma attached to women who instead pursued educational or career ambitions was too high a price to pay.

As those social pressures eased, a seismic shift began to occur. According to the U.S. Department of Education, starting in 1982, a larger proportion of women than men began earning bachelor's and master's degrees. By 2016, women are projected to earn 60% of bachelor's, 63% of master's and 54% of doctorate and professional degrees.[4] If the trend holds, a majority of people with college degrees in the U.S. will be women.

Many other countries are experiencing a similar trend. As early as 2007, UNESCO reported that women accounted for more than half of university graduates in countries like China and Brazil, and that there were three women for every two men graduating from tertiary education in Malaysia, Philippines, Thailand and Uruguay.[5]

As we'll discuss in more detail later, increased success in education is also translating into more jobs — at least at the entry level. Numbers vary with industry and country, but in general women now consistently make up 50% or more of the workforce.

The percentage of women drops significantly, however, as we go up the corporate ladder. This isn't because women lack ambition by nature, or are unwilling to do what it takes to become senior executives. But we do need to look at ambition and career planning more closely to understand why a "glass ceiling" still exists, and how to help women break through.

"She lacks personal vision" and "she can't articulate what she wants from her career" are common complaints I hear from executives, mostly men, who are trying to develop succession planning for high-performing women and increase the number of women in their leadership pipeline. I tell them I understand their hesitation to invest time and money developing individuals who seem unsure of what they want. However, I also point out that there are understandable, and surmountable, reasons *why* many women seem unsure or haven't invested much time in determining what they want or how to get there.

Quite a few women in these situations have told me that the "how can we advance your career?" conversation caught them by surprise. In an ideal world, such conversations would be the expected outcome for *any* employee who had proven competency, put in the appropriate years of experience, and demonstrated an ability to get things done. But in most women's observations and experiences, hard work and talent often do *not* translate into career advancement. The paltry percentage of women in most upper management positions bears witness to the accuracy of that perception. So we should not be surprised that the "career advancement" conversation often evokes a response like "I never thought they had a vision of me at that level" or "I saw so many women ask and walk away empty-handed, I had given up aspiring or planning for more."

There is a vicious cycle here. In part because they see evidence of an achievement gap in the workforce, women cede ambition — a quality that most cultures already discourage in females from day one. Yet, as Facebook COO Sheryl Sandberg pointed out in a 2011 interview with Charlie Rose, "until women are as ambitious as men, they're not going to achieve as much as men."[6]

Breaking this cycle on the societal level will be a long, slow process. Educational systems and cultural norms have a long way to go before we can expect women to embrace ambition with zest and no fear of social retribution. Social scientists have pointed out that even manufacturers of toys and other products will need to reconsider their implicit and explicit messaging.

In the meantime, I have four suggestions for companies that want to help women be more forward-looking and craft long-term plans to manage and sustain their careers:

- Realize that women in your organization aren't "incapable" of ambition, but may need more support and encouragement to develop, express, and act on it. I will offer more tips on this important point at the end of the chapter, and return to this subject throughout the book.

- Get the "ambition dialogue" out front early. The sooner a woman knows you view her as a potential leader, the more likely she will be to see herself that way and begin planning accordingly.

- Make sure that promising women are actively mentored. Research by Catalyst in 2008 found that 78% of men were actively mentored by a CEO or senior executive, compared to 69% of women. Those numbers are no doubt closer than they would have been two decades ago, but that's still a noteworthy gap — particularly since, for the reasons we've described, women are more likely to need such support to succeed.

- Do not force women to see career and family as an either/or choice. This undermines ambition and discourages long-term career planning. Instead, make family options part of the discussion from the start. If you believe in a woman's long-term value and leadership potential for your organization, it's not hard to justify a two-month maternity leave (or even two years as exists in some European countries) to retain her. Technology has also made it much easier to keep someone actively engaged with the organization even while on leave.

Career ambition isn't a genetic trait that males have and females don't — it's a mindset that develops with recognition, encouragement, positive and timely feedback, strategic support, and mentoring. When women receive that from family, teachers, society, senior managers, and other role models, they are better able to explore and express ambition as a desirable attribute. Unfortunately, many women you manage will *not* have had those advantages — and their sense of ambition will not develop overnight. Unless we make a concerted effort to help them carve out a clear career path, understand the consequences of limiting self-talk and its impact on self-promoting, and look towards the future with optimism and purpose, they will continue to derail.

The misconception that ambition is just not a female quality must be replaced by the understanding that it is a trait that can and should be developed. This isn't just a humanistic issue, it's a business challenge. The number of women in the workforce continues to grow, yet many companies don't have an effective support system in place to ensure their presence, engagement and promotion through the ranks. As a result, retention, productivity, and the strength of the leadership pipeline all suffer.

Misconception 3: Women Can Be Paid Less Than Men

Women have been working outside the home in large numbers since the 19th century. In the U.S., legislation to limit working hours and improve working conditions for women and children began appearing early in the 20th century, but not until the 1960s did federal laws attempt to improve the economic and legal status of women. Most notably, the Civil Rights Act of 1964 prohibited discrimination against women by any company with 25 or more employees — and the Equal Pay Act of 1963 required women and men to receive equal pay for equal work.

Nearly 50 years later, "equal pay for equal work" is still not a reality. Analyzing data from the 1950s and 1960s, we find that women earned on average about 59 to 64 cents for every dollar their male counterparts earned.[7] The numbers have improved — but still fall far short of equal. According to the 2011 Fact Sheet from the Institute for Women's Policy Research, "the ratio of women's and men's median annual earnings for full-time year-round workers in the U.S. was 77.4 in 2010, less than half a percentage point higher than in 2009."[8]

In other words, in the U.S., women still get paid about 23% less than men for the same jobs. This inequality touches almost all industries and professions. Catalyst's August 2012 publication "Women's Earnings and Income" reports that female doctors make about $12,000 less per year than their male counterparts, females make just over 70.5% of males in the financial services industry, 73.8% in manufacturing, 76% in wholesale and retail trade, and so on.[9] The National Association of Women Lawyers reports that there is about a $70,000 annual gap between female and male law firm equity partners.[10]

Data from other countries shows that this challenge is universal, with wage gaps ranging from about 9% to 20% in most of the European Union, Canada and Australia, up to 28% in Japan and 39% in Korea.[11]

There are many reasons that your company should take proactive measures to ensure pay equity: It is the right thing to do, enhances your reputation, makes the company more attractive for both men and women, and reduces legal liability. In one of the more high-profile cases in the latter area, three former female employees sued Goldman Sachs for systematic discrimination against women, including compensating them less than their male counterparts.

Here's one more reason that is close to the heart of this book: Unequal compensation sends a message of devaluing women's work, which can erode self-worth, kill morale, and disincentivize promising female employees from pursuing greater responsibility and contributing to their full potential. Conversely, equal compensation helps increase self-confidence, promotes a sense of belonging and being valued, and inspires stronger commitment and performance. If you want to attract and retain top female talent, your company must send an unequivocal message that it respects women's contributions and will promote and compensate them equally to men.

Companies that send that message are still rare — and therefore gain a competitive advantage. To illustrate the point further, I recently had dinner with a group of female executives, each of whom had received well-earned promotions. Only *one* was satisfied with the financial package offered to her. The rest had essentially been told to be happy with the promotion and be patient about financial rewards. So, even in top positions, women are still hearing a devaluing message: Working hard may get you a promotion, but not the compensation to match your new responsibilities. You don't need a crystal ball to predict which woman at that dinner is likely to be a high performer for her organization for years to come and which women are more likely to "walk away" one day.

Pay inequity can impact corporate as well as personal performance. For example, a top-tier female executive I know had been given an important position and asked to recharge the performance of a highly specialized team of professionals. She was excited about leading the way toward improvements and her abilities kicked into high gear. Then one day, the salary and compensation package of her male predecessor accidentally got mixed in with those of her direct reports — revealing that he had been paid $15,000 more for the same job. When she approached HR about the discrepancy, the response she got was "well, that is what you accepted." The message once again: Do an exceptional job and we'll advance you into more challenging roles, but don't expect to be valued the same as a male peer. This woman confided to me that the experience really took the wind out of her sails at exactly the time she needed her confidence and energy to get her team reorganized and push a new agenda through.

Why are such pay inequalities still the norm? One contributing factor is the misconception that a woman's salary is supplemental to the household income rather than primary. Consciously or unconsciously, if you believe that Joe's entire family depends on him while Mary's income is just a nice extra, you may be more likely to hire Joe, promote him faster, or find a way to compensate him better.

Like other beliefs we've discussed so far, that reasoning is seriously flawed in today's economy. *The World's Women 2010*, a report published by the U.N., notes that women's workforce participation globally has held steady at around 52% since 1990, while male participation has been dropping.[12] Other data shows that in many countries more women have become primary or sole breadwinners, and in any case represent an increasing percentage of household income. To cite one example, a report by the U.S. Congress titled *Women and the Economy 2010* says that "wives' earnings play an increasingly important role in families' income. In 1983, wives' incomes comprised just 29% of total family income. By 2008, wives' incomes comprised 36% of total family income."[13]

With women making up a larger percentage of the workforce and contributing a higher percentage of household income, their lower compensation actually translates into decreased purchasing power and spending, which not only impacts individual families but also becomes a drag on the entire economy.

In short, "equal pay for equal work" is more than a legal mandate; it's a smart business and economic strategy. As a senior executive or manager, taking steps to ensure compensation parity is one of the most impacting ways to make a difference for both your organization and the women you hope to advance through your leadership pipeline.

To Remove the Barriers We Must First Acknowledge Them

Men and women alike put on a good show of having moved forward to more progressive and inclusive ways of interacting. But below the surface, the legacies of the misconceptions discussed in this chapter continue to be a negative influence on perceptions and behaviors.

Legislative actions like the Lilly Ledbetter Fair Pay Act of 2009 in the U.S. are fine, but the real change has to happen in corporate practices and expectations — and beyond that, at an individual level. Each challenge discussed in this chapter involves human, psychological, and communication factors that managers like you are in an excellent position to transform for those you manage and throughout your corporate culture.

I should reiterate, however, that I'm not just talking about changing "male perceptions" or implementing new policies in your company. I am also talking about actions to help women overcome internal obstacles.

For example, let's return to our discussion on ambition. A critical first step is to acknowledge that, for most women, there *are* obstacles to embracing, developing and managing ambition that negatively impact their long-term vision, acceleration process, and leadership potential. To get the most out of your female talent, these obstacles must be addressed and removed. We'll explore this as it relates to ambition and other challenges throughout the book, but as promised earlier, here are a few basic tips I give to my clients to help them close the gender ambition gap:

- Create opportunities to talk about future plans with promising female professionals. Keep in mind that it might have to be you who takes the first step in initiating a discussion or introducing the "what ifs" that help her envision development possibilities.
- Promote networking between strong individual contributors, seasoned employees, and key stakeholders. It is especially important for women to have a chance to interact with others throughout the company — networking can help them see their own possibilities more clearly.
- Implement a coaching process to quickly identify areas that need work and develop a plan of action. Coaching relationships, whether internal or through an expert consultant, have a depth, focus and frequency of contact that ensures positive results in a shorter amount of time.

These are good tips for *all* employees — you may even feel you already have them in place. But I would urge you to look closely at whether what you currently do is effective for females as well as males. Ignoring our differences and pretending everyone will respond to the same approach is *not* a path to success.

Now, let's move on to some of the important workforce trends that have shaped today's workplace realities. Like the misconceptions in this chapter, these trends need to be understood in order to truly move forward.

CHAPTER 2
Women and the Workforce: Key Milestones and Trends

Whether you're leading a company, managing a business unit or major initiative, or helping to develop the next generation of managers, you're probably facing a much different and more complex workforce than the one you entered at the start of your career. Multicultural, multigenerational, highly mobile, and hyperconnected through the Internet, today's workforce is not only more diverse, it's more demanding. There are new organizational, behavioral and communication challenges that can't be resolved with past strategies and approaches.

Confronting gender and cultural differences is essential to moving forward. Unfortunately, many men and women alike have the attitude that there have been enough legal and HR initiatives over the past couple decades, so if challenges still exist, it's now on the individual to step up. In my experience, when this attitude prevails, both individuals and the organization become "stuck" in the same old struggles. The more effective mindset is to engage individuals throughout the organization in a dialogue about why previous efforts have not paid off, and what can be done to better understand, adapt and thrive in the new economy.

Attracting, developing and integrating the unique talents and contributions of women isn't just a corporate challenge — in most countries, it's a societal one. Reports such as the U.N.'s *The World's Women 2010* make it clear that although there has been progress in areas like education and workforce participation, women still have limited access to positions of corporate or political power, gender pay parity remains elusive, and women continue to bear almost exclusive responsibility for the additional work of raising children and housekeeping.[14]

You may be more focused on keeping your company competitive and improving business performance than changing the world, but it's important to understand the scope of the challenge — and the potential rewards. Gender-smart, culturally sensitive companies (and countries) consistently achieve better performance in a range of categories: economic growth, profitability, cultural stability, personal satisfaction, and even healthcare costs!

My work revolves around helping executives, companies and individuals to realize that potential. But to do that, we must first understand aspects of the past and ongoing trends that are shaping both the present and the immediate future. That is the focus of this chapter.

World War II: Working Women Excel, Then Get Sent Home

When I began to research this book, I realized that World War II was a critical milestone: a period when the misconception that women are "the weaker sex" was put to the test and proven wrong. There is value in revisiting this historical moment, remembering how women performed, and considering the possible parallels with their strategic importance in today's environment.

When the U.S. entered the war, demand for manufacturing output increased, but manpower decreased due to military deployment. Women stepped right in to build and manufacture the goods needed by the nation and its military.

As Susan Hartmann points out in *The Home Front and Beyond: American Women in the 1940s*, patriotism influenced these women, but it was ultimately economic motives that convinced many to enter the workforce, in some cases for the first time. Once there, they quickly discovered the intangible benefits of work as well: learning new skills, aiding the public good, and proving that they could be capable contributors to the nation's economic development and well-being.[15]

The biggest challenge for women as they entered the workforce was dealing with the misperceptions and resistance of men accustomed to working in male-only environments. A 1943 *Transportation Magazine* guide to hiring women, for example, advised supervisors to "pick married women because they are more committed and less flirtatious." If hiring older women, the advice was to find those with previous work experience — otherwise they would be "cantankerous and fussy." The guide also recommended hiring "those who are husky [because] they seem to be more even tempered" and counseled that "women need an adequate number of rest periods. It makes sense for the female psychology."[16]

Women overcame such stereotypes, consistently revealing not only a strong commitment and work ethic, but also an innate capacity to learn quickly, rise to on-the-job challenges, and successfully juggle parenting and work. Along the way, they earned the respect of the men they worked with — yet were still sent back out of the workforce once the war ended. This is captured well in remembrances collected at the National Park Service's online exhibit, *Rosie the Riveter: Women Working During World War II*. One of my favorites is by Delana Jensen Close, who worked as a machinist:

> "V-E Day...was a day of celebration, but one of mixed emotions for us. We lost our jobs....[W]hen the foreman of my section shook my hand and said goodbye, he added, 'You were the best man I had.' "[17]

As an article elsewhere on the exhibit explains, "After the war, the cultural division of labor by sex reasserted itself. Many women remained in the workforce but employers forced them back into lower-paying female jobs. Most women were laid off and told to go back to their homes."[18]

They did just that, believing it was patriotic to make space for the men who had been fighting. But working in manufacturing during the war years began a shift in how women's roles and value were perceived in terms of the workforce. Women had proven to their mostly male employers that they could do more than be housewives. Just as importantly, many women had made a psychological shift themselves. The opportunities they'd experienced during the war had given them a broader sense of individuality and independence.

The iconic "Rosie the Riveter" images used to recruit women into the workforce during World War II continue to offer a good lesson in valuing gender differences. Rosie is undeniably feminine — she is pretty, wears makeup and has her nails done. Yet she is just as undeniably strong and determined, with no fear or weakness. She has a direct, unequivocal attitude that shows she understands what needs to be done and what is at stake.

Unfortunately, as women began returning to the workforce in larger numbers a generation later, the image of Rosie had been replaced by a new schema: "mirroring" the male behaviors that dominated corporate culture. For most women, I believe this has created a contextual challenge — a battle rather than harmony between their femininity and professional persona. Individual women and managers alike would do well to revisit what we can learn from Rosie. Women will not realize their full potential as professionals by compromising their identity *as* women. It was by honoring *all* of who she was, including her gender differences, that Rosie proved "I *can* do it"!

In the coaching work my firm does, the first step toward transforming behavior and leveraging strengths is to guide each woman to explore and reflect on her authentic self. What makes her unique? How does she see herself? What are her aspirations? Is she comfortable in her skin — and if not, what needs to change to achieve that comfort?

We start by recognizing and validating individual differences, then look at how personal skills and qualities can be better leveraged for performance and successful interactions. Similarly, we use exercises in self-awareness, emotional intelligence, personality, and other qualities to help women find a leadership style that aligns with who they truly are. Too often, managers and women get stuck in a "one-shape-fits-all" mentality. Trying to "shed" differences, they jettison real strengths in the process. For the individual and the organization, that's a recipe for failure in the 21st century workplace.

Changes in Family Planning — and Career Planning

The topic of birth control inspires strong emotions, so I want to emphasize from the start that this section has no political agenda. Regardless of our personal or religious views, from a business standpoint, we simply can't ignore the extraordinary impact that increased access, use and effectiveness of birth control has had on women in the workforce.

In particular, the invention and popularization of the birth control pill was a significant turning point. By giving women the power to choose if and when they became pregnant, it also enhanced their ability to pursue education, invest more time in career development, and engage in long-term planning. Suddenly a wide range of professional careers became feasible.

Women's increased control over their futures and careers launched other trends that still impact men and women alike. For example, there has been a decline in marriage and a corresponding increase in social and/or family units other than traditional marriage. As seen in the chart below, those who do marry are also waiting longer:

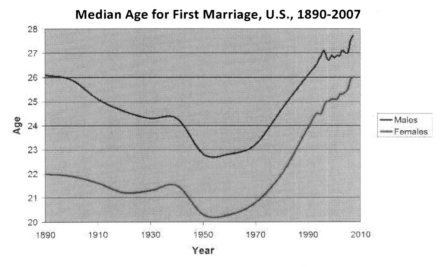

Median Age for First Marriage, U.S., 1890-2007

(Source: U.S. Bureau of the Census)

In a corresponding trend, couples are also waiting longer to have children. The major implication for women in the workforce is that they have been able to put off, and *are* putting off, marriage and children until they have established themselves in careers.

This presents a challenge — and opportunity — for companies. More women, especially younger women, now evaluate career options with an eye toward "wanting it all": time for work and time for parenting. Some companies are distinguishing themselves as employers of choice, and earning long-term employee loyalty, by adapting in ways that make that possible. Others still structured along traditional lines may make women feel forced to make a choice: either a career with the company or having children. In fact, just recently I talked with a woman who, at 24, had already decided that she couldn't have children because her career path didn't allow room for it!

Companies that force women to make this choice are being short-sighted in numerous respects. Most obviously, you will lose some of your best women (and fail to attract top talent to your company in the first place) if you make it impossible to integrate family planning with work planning. As I remind my corporate clients, women are not pregnant forever. A few months of leave, flex time and related benefits are small investments compared to losing committed employees and then spending time and money to hire and train replacements. Not having a family-friendly workplace also creates scheduling stress for men and women alike, which can hurt morale and productivity.

Moving toward a family-friendly workplace does not necessarily require a major initiative or radical restructuring. Every company is different and should find solutions that make sense for its people and the nature of its business operations. If providing on-site daycare makes sense for you, great. But companies can win and retain female talent just by offering well-structured maternity leave and benefits, flex time or telecommuting options, and a culture where everyone from the C-suite and HR department through all levels of management clearly supports women who want to have families rather than subtly punishing them or treating them as a liability.

There are benefits for everyone in shifting to a more family-friendly, accommodating culture and management style. The company gets the competitive edge of attracting and retaining top female talent, and, as we'll see later in this chapter, also positions itself better for the Millennial generation now advancing through the workforce. A more open dialogue about family planning aids managers in long-term strategic planning and in developing effective short-term solutions while someone is on maternity leave. And individual women, rather than feeling that there is an all-or-nothing choice between family and career, can find a "middle way" that allows fulfillment and success in both areas. Indeed, one piece of advice I give to both the managers and individual women I work with is to leverage today's technology to keep women engaged and productive throughout maternity leave. This can be especially important in European countries where leave times may be years rather than months.

There's one other related issue worth mentioning. The accessibility and effectiveness of modern birth control combined with the struggle to compete in male-driven corporate cultures is causing many women to choose to be childless, particularly in the most developed countries. Europe is experiencing a below-replacement fertility rate, meaning zero or near zero population growth. Japan's population is contracting. The U.S. could be headed in a similar direction. A chart from the Pew Research Center shows the percentage of women who are still childless between the ages of 40 and 44 nearly doubling since 1976:

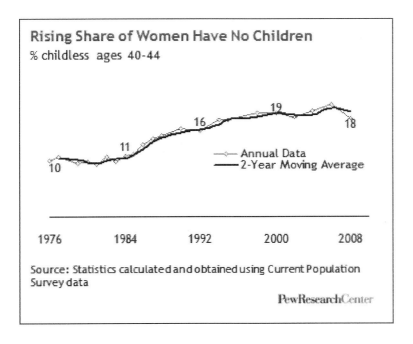

On first glance, some might be tempted to see this as a positive. After all, not having children removes one of the challenges that prevent corporations from advancing women into positions of power, right?

But step back and look at the big picture. More women in the workforce and zero population growth is a formula for corporate and national vulnerability. Where will your future workforce and leaders come from if local populations are stagnant or shrinking? Even in challenging economic circumstances, some countries have already had to spend resources recruiting and importing workers from elsewhere because of workforce shortages. Bottom line, forcing women to choose between family and career exacts too high a cost for all involved: individual women, businesses, and the community.

The Confusion of "Equal" and Ongoing Quest for *Fair*

One of the most tangible achievements of the Civil Rights movement was passing the Civil Rights Act of 1964, including Title VII forbidding job discrimination based on race, color, religion, sex, or national origin. However, the Equal Employment Opportunity Commission (EEOC) did little at first to enforce Title VII as it applied to women. This increased a perceived need to fight for women's rights separately, and in 1966 a group of 28 women at the Third Annual Conference on the Status of Women founded the National Organization for Women (NOW) to do so. By the end of the year, NOW had 300 members; by the end of the century, it had a half million.

Through organizations such as NOW, women began to demand changes in discriminatory laws. They also started to seek the right to be heard as individuals. Women were no longer satisfied with defining their status in society in terms of marriage and caregiving. They wanted more.

The Civil Rights Act and EEOC have enabled a great deal of progress for women and minorities alike in the U.S., but I believe the resulting paradigm also created serious misconceptions and challenges. In particular, the discourse became so dominated by literal uses of the word "equality" that we lost the deeper intention of the law — as well as the ability to appreciate the value of gender differences.

While legal equality is a worthy goal, too many women mistakenly pursued a notion of equality that meant emulating traditional male behaviors. Rough and tough was the perceived acceptable conduct to ensure corporate advancement. Women who decided to have a family and children felt that qualities valued in their role of wife and mother had to be erased the moment they walked into the office on Monday morning.

For both women and minorities, trying to be equal to — in the sense of being the *same as* — white men has rarely paid off in either career success or personal fulfillment. This approach has also constrained the growth and success of businesses and organizations by eliminating or muting the *different* attributes and qualities that make women and minorities complementary, strategic partners.

To unlock the potential of both individuals and organizations, I believe we must shift our paradigm from equality/sameness to *fairness*. This concept has been articulated in various ways by thinkers from all walks of life in recent decades, and I am convinced that it is fundamental to helping women ascend to higher positions in the workforce.

A simple definition of fairness is "the ability to make judgment free from discrimination or dishonesty." Achieving that standard, rather than mere appearances of "equality," demands the development of a work environment that:

- Supports the exchange of ideas with respect and interest in others
- Celebrates the value of diverse backgrounds and cultural contexts
- Encourages individuals to use and develop inherent qualities and abilities rather than trying to assimilate
- Promotes inclusive thinking and behaviors
- Focuses on measuring, encouraging and rewarding real talent and performance
- Eliminates the quota mentality and demoralizing role of women and minorities as token figures

An emphasis on "sameness" and assimilation results in the loss of complementary attributes associated with women and minorities — like exploring multiple perspectives, focusing on collaboration rather than competition, and developing empathy and trust. These are all proving to be highly valuable attributes in achieving more profitable organizations.

University of Michigan Professor Scott E. Page and economist Lu Hong from Chicago Loyola University even developed a mathematical model that reinforces the claims of other researchers that diverse groups can solve complex business problems better that homogeneous groups. In fact, in "Groups of Diverse Problem Solvers Can Outperform Groups of High-Ability Problem Solvers," they show that, in certain circumstances, "diversity can trump ability."[19]

An article from Stanford University's Graduate School of Business titled "Diverse Backgrounds and Personalities Can Strengthen Groups" cites similar findings by professor Margaret A. Neale. The article explains that after reviewing 50 years of related research, Neale found that "diversity across dimensions, such as functional expertise, education or personality, can increase performance by enhancing creativity or group problem-solving." It also quotes Neale as saying "the mere presence of diversity you can see, such as a person's race or gender, actually cues a team in that there's likely to be differences of opinion" which can "enhance the team's ability to handle conflict, because members expect it and are not surprised when it surfaces."[20]

Conversely, when women and minorities strive merely to "act like white men" — and leaders intentionally or unintentionally hold them to that impossible standard — the result is confusion throughout the organization. Women and minorities are left asking: What am I doing wrong? What more do I need to do to be treated fairly? Are my natural attributes getting in the way of my success?

In my experience, the same challenge exists in markets worldwide. Men and women are still searching for a way to be themselves and develop a sense of normalcy in daily work interactions. The "equality agenda" may have been a necessary first step on that road — but the next step requires that we upshift our thinking to fairness.

I cannot emphasize enough that, even aside from humanistic concerns, superior business performance depends on understanding and embracing our complementary differences.

Gender *and* Culture: The Reality of a Diverse Workforce

The workforce is growing more diverse — and will continue to diversify well into the future. The surge of women into the workforce is part of that — but we are also seeing a rapidly changing population mix. The following graph provides a good snapshot of the shift in the U.S.:

Figure 1. In the U.S., the white portion of the working-age population (ages 25 to 64) is declining, while the minority portion is increasing.

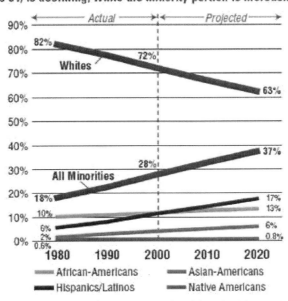

Notes: Population projections are based on historical rates of change for immigration, birth, and death. Pacific Islanders are included with Asian-Americans. Alaska Natives are included with Native Americans. Projections for Native Americans are based on 1990 Census. The Census category "other races" is not included.

Sources: U.S. Census Bureau, 5% Public Use Microdata Samples (based on 1980, 1990, and 2000 Census) and U.S. Population Projections (based on 2000 Census).

Similarly, data from the U.S. Census Bureau suggests that two thirds of population growth between now and 2050 will be due to immigration. Combining such data with projections by the Bureau of Labor Statistics, Mitra Toossi gives us a detailed picture of the future workforce in an article that appeared in *Monthly Labor Review*. Hispanics are projected to be 24.3% of the total workforce by 2050, growing at an average 2% every year. The Asian population is expected to grow at a similar annual rate and reach 8.3% by 2050. The African-American segment will grow at a slower rate, 1% annually, and become 14% of the workforce over the same period, while the white non-Hispanic portion of the workforce decreases from nearly 70% in 2005 to around 50% by 2050.[21]

Globally, we see a similar trend. As the U.N. graph below shows, between 2000 and 2050 populations in developed markets are expected to

remain stable or decline. Drilling a bit deeper into the data, we see expo-
nential growth in Africa, China and India.

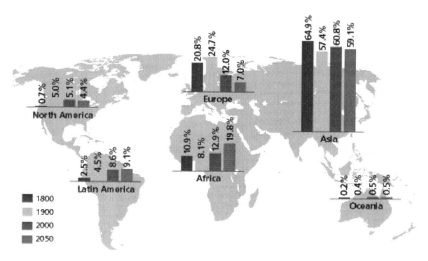

Source: U.N. Data, World Population Prospects

For large corporations in particular, it is clear that you will depend on
a more culturally diverse workforce in the future. That adds complexity
and increases potential conflicts for you as a manager. In my work, I regularly
hear concerns about this — and the mistaken assumption, as with women
in the workforce, that the "outsiders" must conform to existing models.
On the contrary, change must be a two-way street — it is a strategic imperative for companies to adapt to the new workforce.

As a senior executive or manager, you are on the front lines of this
change. It is important to understand and anticipate the challenges of a
diverse workforce for everyone and to help bridge the inevitable gaps that
will occur for team members. If you do, you will transform the potential conflicts of diversity into rich opportunities to improve business performance.

Youth Factor: Generation X, Millennials and Women Share Values, Work Styles

Generational diversity is another trend impacting the makeup of the
workforce. This is especially pronounced in countries like the U.S., where,

arguably for the first time in history, four distinct generations now regularly work side by side:

- Veterans (born before 1946, but often remaining in the workforce well past traditional retirement age)
- Baby Boomers (born 1946-1964)
- Generation X (born 1964-1980)
- Millennials or Generation Y (born 1980-2000)

Differing values, learning styles, attitudes and expectations between these generations can create workforce tensions and management challenges. Knowledge transfer is one that has received much attention as organizations scramble to make sure there is no "brain drain" or loss of institutional knowledge as Veterans and Baby Boomers retire. But, with few exceptions, almost *every* area of business performance involves an interdependence between these generations. Leaders and managers who can tap the different strengths of each cohort and inspire multigenerational collaboration will succeed; those limited to the perspective of their own generation will struggle, and find their teams struggling as well.

In the context of this book, what I find most interesting is how often the expectations and needs of Generation X and the Millennials mirror those that women have been seeking for more than 40 years.

Both younger generations, particularly the Millennials, demand greater self-determination in the workplace. Having often witnessed the negative impacts of "the rat race," they are less likely to embrace traditional expressions of drive and ambition. That's not to say they aren't capable of commitment and excellent performance — but they need more incentive than just "getting ahead." Striking a balance between work and personal life is critically important to them — including wanting more flexibility with regard to work time and better family leave benefits.

For example, in a recent meeting with a New York law firm, a 28-year-old male lawyer told me he was the first male lawyer at his firm to ask for "flex" leave to be with his wife during and after the birth of their child. He said the firm's managing partners seemed a bit shocked by the request. This is an excellent example of what has changed with the new generation. "Maternity leave" is being replaced by "parental leave" as it becomes clear that having time for family and child-raising isn't just a "female issue" — it's a value shared by young men as well.

Similarly, the head of HR at a global law firm recently told me that "flex time" requests have expanded far beyond women trying to balance family and career. Reinforcing the point about younger generations seeking to balance work and, as she put it, "private life," she told me that even inexperienced staff fresh out of law school had no hesitancy in asking for extra vacation, time off to visit with family or attend a friend's wedding, and so on. This experience was new to her — the firm's culture had always revolved around a "non-stop" work ethic where it wasn't unusual to put in long hours six or seven days a week. Prioritizing "private life" was a foreign concept — but, as she acknowledged, also one likely to play a prominent role in where the best and brightest Millennials choose to work.

Senior executives and managers may understandably feel disoriented or outright threatened by the sense that corporate policies and norms that have held sway for decades are under attack. Millennials *are* actively challenging, and often winning changes to, everything from flex time and benefits packages to the structure of the work environment, and even basic definitions of talent and performance. Indeed, a comfort with constant change is one of the generation's most distinctive traits, along with a pronounced focus on individuality and self-realization and a need for immediate reward. The impact of these traits on short-term and long-term decision-making is significant — Millennials, far more than any previous generation, feel they should choose their employer rather than the other way around.

This is not to say we should throw up our hands and do whatever the Millennials want. But, as with changes driven by gender and cultural diversity, companies that adapt and strike a balance between the traditional and the new stand to gain a competitive edge on numerous levels, including having more committed, loyal employees. The process of adapting is somewhat simplified, and the benefits are multiplied, by a point I mentioned earlier: Schedule flexibility, sensitivity to family life, and many other areas that attract and retain top female talent will also make you an employer of choice for promising Millennials. The following table, based on the work of Claire Raines, highlights a few key parallels. Naturally, not "every" Millennial or woman shares these traits, but they are common enough to be worth consideration as you develop a strategy to address their needs, win their loyalty, and leverage their talents:

Women and Millennials

Women	Millennials
Collaborative; enjoy working in groups	Through social media, have a comfort with group dynamics and multicultural differences
Want to balance family and career	Seek work-life balance and employers that accommodate that balance
Ability to multitask	Multitasking is a natural operating mode
Look for recognition of job well done	Want immediate praise, gratification and rewards
Empathetic, personally flexible	Thrive in flexible environments, comfortable with constant change
Time management skills (and challenges) related to juggling multiple roles	Desire to do tasks efficiently in order to free up more time for other pursuits
Motivated by meaningful work and stretch assignments	Need to be challenged; seek new and uncharted opportunities

Source: Based on material from GenerationsAtWork.com
by Claire Raines Associates

In short, environments and management styles geared to welcome and motivate women will also welcome and motivate Millennials. Obviously, good management requires a complementary approach that can reach *all* the groups in your diverse workforce. But there is good reason to focus special attention on women and Millennials: They are the future of the workforce. As Veterans and Baby Boomers retire, Generation X, Millennials and women will continue to make up a larger percentage of employees and potential leaders. These groups are integral to succession planning — developing depth now can strengthen your competitive position for years to come.

"Lehman Brothers & Sisters": The Case for Gender-Balanced Leadership

In a February 2009 column for *The New York Times*, Nicholas D. Kristof wrote of the 2009 World Economic Forum in Davos, Switzerland that "some of the most interesting discussions revolved around whether we would be in the same mess today if Lehman Brothers had been Lehman Sisters. The consensus...is that the optimal bank would have been Lehman Brothers and Sisters." Identifying Wall Street as "one of the most male-dominated bastions in the business world," he then cites the work of Page and Hong on diversity, as well as a British study linking testosterone levels to risk-taking. He asks an important question: Does male-only leadership result in "second-rate decision-making?"[22]

Professor Michel Ferrary from France's CERAM Business School (now SKEMA) has explored similar territory. Analyzing companies from the French CAC 40 stock exchange index, he found that the more women were present in management positions, the less their share prices fell in 2008. Noting gender studies that have shown that women behave and manage differently from men — including being "more risk-averse" and having more of "a long-term perspective" — he too concludes that there is a need for gender-balanced leadership teams.[23]

Similarly, "Groundbreakers: Using the Strength of Women to Rebuild the World Economy", an oft-cited Ernst & Young report from 2009, touted the broad range of studies that have examined the relationship between corporate financial performance and the presence of women in leadership roles and concluded that "having more women at the top improves financial performance."[24]

None of these sources suggest abolishing male leadership styles — but, like an increasing number of researchers and business management experts, they *are* pointing out the benefits of a balanced approach that taps the different, complementary strengths of male and female qualities.

In light of other workforce trends, such balance is becoming a necessity. The top-down management style seems less effective every day, at least when it's the *only* style. Telling people what to do works for short periods of time, and in certain contexts, but for large segments of today's workforce it inspires mistrust, resentment and resistance. Knowledge workers hired for their expertise, for example, tend to need to be seen and treated as equals. They prefer to be consulted and asked for opinions, not directed — hallmarks of the collaborative leadership style more common among women.

The global economic crisis may have put a spotlight on the limits of the traditional male-only leadership paradigm, but researchers have long understood the shortcomings of homogeneous "group think" in general. Groups comprised of people who think alike naturally tend to be comfortable with each other and reach decisions with ease. But therein lies the problem — with no other perspectives represented, decisions are seldom subject to thorough analysis, in-depth questioning or challenge. Better decision-making, like innovation or quality improvement or other areas of business performance, flourishes when we prioritize positive change over the comfort of the status quo. In the case of decision-making, that means learning to see traditional male leadership qualities, such as determination, pushing hard and competing, as just one part of a more strategically diverse, collaborative, democratized approach.

Crisis provokes change — and in organizations, that usually implies a change in leadership. In light of the economic crisis and its causes, it is not surprising that increasing the presence of women in leadership has become a hot topic. But in another sense this is problematic: Too often, women get the green light to the C-suite only when companies are faced with insurmountable problems. For example, Xerox asked Anne M. Mulcahy to become CEO in 2001, when the company was on the brink of filing for bankruptcy.

In fact, elevating women to positions of power under precarious circumstances is so prevalent that two researchers, Michelle Ryan and Alex Haslam from the University of Exeter, coined a name for it: the "Glass Cliff."[25] Among a number of interesting studies on this phenomenon, they asked 83 business leaders to pick a new financial director for a hypothetical company whose performance was declining. The participants, who had preferred male leadership and rated male leadership performance higher than females in other facets of the study, shifted to choosing a female

candidate when the company was in crisis. There are multiple explana-
tions for this tendency, but it's hard not to read the result as, "if
someone's going to take a fall, we might as well let it be a woman."[26]

Whether out of obligation, gratitude that they're finally getting a
leadership role, or both, women regularly take on these risky clean-up
jobs. Taking control of a ship that's already half sunk is hardly ideal for
showcasing one's talent, but so far it is one of the few ways women get a
chance to demonstrate their leadership skills without resistance.

The important question for all of us, however, is why do we wait for a
crisis before tapping those skills? If women prove themselves exceptional
under duress, how much more could they contribute if given the reins
under normal circumstances?

There is a strong business case for proactively developing and promoting
women in order to achieve the more balanced "Lehman Brothers and Sisters"
leadership team recommended by the "wise white men" at Davos. Give
women the same opportunities as men, the same levels of support, the
same access to social and strategic networks, the same path to the C-suite,
and it's not just the women who benefit, it's the entire organization.

"The Feminine Mystique" Cedes to a Fem-Momentum

The role of women has changed radically in the nearly 50 years since
Betty Friedan wrote *The Feminine Mystique*. Legacies from the societal
myth that a woman's fulfillment should come solely from her role as
mother and housewife remain, but the new reality is better expressed by
the title of a *Harvard Business Review* article by Michael J. Silverstein and
Kate Sayre: "The Female Economy." As the first sentence of this article
concisely explains: "Women now drive the world economy." The article
points out that women control $20 trillion in annual consumer spending
and have a yearly earning potential of $13 trillion.[27]

In their book *Inside Her Pretty Little Head*, Jane Cunningham and
Philippa Roberts report other powerful numbers showing that women
have become major economic players:

- In the U.S., women make close to 80% of all consumer
  purchasing decisions

- Women account for 70% of new business start-ups in Canada
- In the U.K., women are projected to control 60% of all personal wealth by 2025
- Women earn 40% of the world's GDP[28]

As we've pointed out in other parts of Section I, women make up more than 50% of graduates with bachelor's and master's degrees. They are half of the global workforce and a growing percentage of the workforce in most countries. Catherine Rampell and many others have even referred to the most recent recession as a "mancession" because in general it hit men harder than women.

There's no way around it: As a manager, you will hire, work with, and develop more women than ever before. They will be a key source of new talent and, as we've shown, their presence at the highest levels of leadership creates more gender-balanced decision-making that can mitigate risk and enhance overall performance. And, unlike the surge of women in the workforce during World War II, this time there is no foreseeable event that would reverse the trend. Women have become a critical strategic variable for the growth and stability of any 21st century business.

From my own work, I can attest that the global corporate dialogue is slowly but surely becoming feminized as more people recognize that it's imperative to look at economic and business development from a balanced perspective that includes men and women. For several years now, most of my consulting work has focused on multinational companies in Europe and the U.S. who are making a conscious strategic effort to attract and retain female talent and enhance their presence in the leadership pipeline.

While many leaders I work with are personally committed to understanding gender and cultural differences better and creating workplace environments that are more fair and representative, what ultimately drives these changes is performance.

Past and ongoing research continues to offer persuasive evidence that creating a balanced, gender-smart work environment is just good business:

- "Women Matter: Gender Diversity, a Corporate Performance Driver", McKinsey's groundbreaking 2007 study of 89 publicly traded companies with market capitalizations of 150 million euros or more, showed that those with the highest levels of gender diversity had higher returns on equity, operating results and stock price growth than their sector averages over a three-year period.[29]

- A Catalyst study of Fortune 500 companies found that companies in the highest quartile of female board directors outperformed those in the lowest quartile by 66% in return on invested capital, 53% in return on equity, and 42% in return on sales.[30]
- "Gender Inequality, Growth and Global Aging," a report from Goldman Sachs, suggested that gender equality in the workforce could increase gross domestic product by 9% in the U.S., 13% in the Eurozone, and 16% in Japan.[31]

Whether we're talking about a nation, a company, or your career as an executive, clinging to the old paradigm will increasingly put you at a disadvantage. As Valerie Hudson concludes in an article for *Foreign Policy,* "the macho cult is gone." She adds that "the answer is not to hand over ultimate power to women. But there is good reason to think that collective decision-making between men and women is the way to go."[32]

Men and women must co-create a new working context — and managers like you must lead the way. I wrote this book to help you see the big picture and remove the obstacles that prevent more effective gender and cultural balance in the workforce. Leveraging gender and cultural differences to develop the potential of your entire workforce is the path to success. Ignore them, and you may find yourself on the scrapheap of thousands of other companies throughout history that failed to adapt to changing market conditions.

SECTION I
Reflections, Exercises, Tips and Takeaways

Reflections:
- How do you view women? Can you see how some of the misconceptions discussed in Chapter 1 have impacted your view?
- How do you respond to gender and cultural differences in general? Do you see them as valuable, confusing, frustrating?
- Has this section given you insights toward a new definition of "fair"? What can you do to make your management style and work environment more fair by that new definition?
- Think about specific interactions you've had involving gender or cultural differences. Are there cases where a misconception or misunderstanding caused challenges? As a manager, how could you have handled the situation better?
- How well is your organization positioned with regard to the emerging trends discussed in Chapter 2?
- What is your company doing to enhance the role, presence, and effectiveness of women? If you're not already taking action in this regard, why not?
- How do you show women that you value their work? What can you do better to encourage their development?

Exercises:
- After doing the self-reflection above, ask three people you know (preferably one from work, one family member, and one friend) how they perceive you in the context of these questions. Ask for candid feedback and compare your answers with theirs. The areas of overlap should reinforce your self-assessment. But pay special attention to

any gaps. In addition to revisiting your answers, it may help to follow up with the person who provided a different assessment and dig deeper to understand the issue better. This can become a powerful learning experience for you and give you the constructive feedback necessary to move forward in your professional career while becoming a more effective leader of your entire team — regardless of gender or culture.

- Use the Reflection questions, either individually or as a group, with your department or team. Try to map out the existing terrain when it comes to gender and cultural differences. Are there many gaps between how different team members perceive that terrain? Where are the biggest challenges and what can be done to address them?

Tips:

- You can gain many insights by talking with people who have different experiences than yours. It can be especially enlightening to reach out to people in your organization or friends who travel a lot as part of their work. Invite them to share anecdotes, success stories, and mistakes with regard to gender and cultural differences. Ask about their perceptions of the role of women in other countries they have visited.
- Sometimes companies don't realize they have shortcomings when it comes to gender and culture diversity — because no one has taken the time to look for them. Whether informally or through a more structured initiative, consider auditing the "state of the company" when it comes to the issues discussed in Section I. For example, how many women are in your leadership pipeline? How well do you sponsor and support talented women in your organization? Where is there room for improvement in talent management practices, the hiring process, succession plans, and long-term growth strategies?

- Section 1 of *Can You Afford to Ignore Me?* provides a panoramic view of the evolution of women in the workforce. Keep what you've learned here in mind as you continue to read the rest of the book. When topics resonate, feel challenging, or seem clarifying and actionable, take notes, give yourself time to reflect, and reach out to discuss those topics with others.

Takeaways:

1. There is a high strategic payoff to challenging and correcting misconceptions related to gender:
   - Women will thrive in environments that allow for and promote their unique strengths and capabilities.
   - Ambition is a desirable personal attribute for everyone and drives corporate performance. It's just sound business to develop a supportive environment and dialogue on this topic and help women overcome any obstacles they have in this area.
   - Pay parity is not only the right thing to do, it is a differentiator and helps you stand out as an employer of choice.

2. As they proved during WWII, women can step up to any challenge and excel in performance by embracing rather than suppressing their femininity.

3. Work environments that offer good work/life balance will attract the best and brightest and result in a more committed and loyal workforce.
   - Millennials and women share many similar aspirations and attributes, including the desire to balance personal life and career.

4. Assessing behavior and managing talent with an "everyone is the same" equality schema does not work. We need to reframe the workplace dialogue around the ideal of fairness, respecting and celebrating the attributes that make us different. One size does not fit all.

5. The global workforce is also multicultural. To succeed, companies will need to adopt a more culturally informed and culture-sensitive management approach.

6. The valuable role women can play as leaders has entered mainstream discourse — backed by plenty of statistical evidence. Attributes typically associated with female behavior are desirable traits in the context of meeting 21st century challenges.

7. The number of women earning higher education degrees and entering the workforce continues to increase. Women now comprise about 50% of the workforce in many markets. This trend will continue, making it imperative that companies give women access to development models and tools that will enhance their contributions and help them move into leadership roles.

SECTION II — DIFFERENCES

Understanding the Impact of Gender and Culture on Behavior, Communication and Business Performance

There are more women in the workforce today than ever before, but in many other respects, there hasn't been much progress since the 1970s. As pointed out in Chapter 1, most countries still have a significant gender wage gap. In the U.S., where women earn about 77% of men for the same work, the gap is closing so slowly that the Institute for Women's Policy Research estimated it will take until 2056 to achieve parity.[33]

Just as disturbingly, despite earning more postgraduate degrees than men, the number of women in leadership positions has also remained relatively stagnant. As a 2010 report by Catalyst put it, "when it comes to top talent, women lag men in advancement, compensation, and career satisfaction. The pipeline is not healthy; inequality remains entrenched." The report, based on a survey of more than 4,000 men and women who had graduated from MBA programs, found that "men were twice as likely as women to get CEO or senior executive positions."[34]

Clearly, the old argument that women just needed more education to catch up to men has not held true. They're also not catching up by mirroring male behavior or embracing "male only" corporate cultures. In fact, as we'll explore in more detail in Chapter 6, most women are caught in a "double bind." If they act "rough and tough" to compete with men, they are distrusted by men *and* women. If they don't, they are perceived as weak and insecure and their contributions are ignored. There is no way to win.

This isn't just bad news for women — it's bad news for companies. In today's highly competitive markets, you need *every* employee to be as engaged and productive as possible. In Chapter 2, we cited data showing the bottom-line value of a more gender-balanced leadership team — but you can't realize that value if you can't figure out how to promote women into the ranks of senior executives. Can you really afford to let your most promising female talent derail?

Many are quick to assert that, if women's progress has stalled, it's not for lack of energy and money spent on efforts to enhance their presence in the workforce and in leadership. It's true that, in addition to legislative efforts in some countries, many companies have diversity initiatives and programs to help women. But what matters is not effort or good intentions, but results. And unless we find and address the root causes of the problem, results will continue to be disappointing.

Institutionalized approaches to managing and developing women all tend to start with a flawed assumption I mentioned in Section I — that "equality" means we must treat everyone, and expect everyone to be, "the same." In effect, we have been tackling the challenges of a two-gender, multicultural workforce from a single-gender, monocultural perspective. By sheer numbers and history, corporate culture evolved around a male perspective. Instead of expanding that model to include a full range of views, we have invested in a futile strategy: reshaping women to fit the male paradigm.

In the past couple decades, scientific research has given us deeper insights into why this approach hasn't worked. Without dismissing overlaps and individual variations, the truth is that there are ways in which women and men are wired differently. They think differently, process emotions differently, and have different strengths when it comes to communication and leadership. If we want both genders, and multiple cultures, to reach their potential and contribute more fully to corporate performance, we have to start by embracing, rather than erasing, these differences.

Unfortunately, it has long been taboo for men and women to consider that brain wiring, hormones and cultural predispositions might lead to differences in how they behave, respond to certain situations, communicate and interact. Many human resources executives readily admit that, often under the advice of their legal team, they have essentially created a code of silence about differences involving gender, race, culture and so on.

Similarly, the quest for political correctness and fear of legal liability have driven companies to strive for "neutral" environments and management practices. The reality of "neutral" hasn't been a *fairer* workplace, however, just one where individuals are constrained by artificial similarities and norms. Worse, we have created a kind of gender/culture black hole that obliterates differences altogether, including those that may be an individual's best strengths.

Asking someone to perform at a higher level and grow into a leader while simultaneously suppressing their differences is like driving a car while stepping on the brake and gas pedals at the same time. With a workforce comprised of a higher and higher percentage of women and people from other cultures, we cannot afford this ineffective approach any longer. This isn't just a humanistic concern — in the global market-place, the ability to strategically leverage gender and culture differences has become a key competitive variable.

There are challenges in transitioning from the outdated "politically correct sameness" framework to an approach that fairly and effectively honors gender, cultural and individual differences. Senior executives and managers like you are instrumental in leading the way — both by creating an environment and processes that factor those differences in, and by acting as a "bridge" between different members of your team to ensure better communications, interactions, and performance.

To do that effectively, you may need to let go of old assumptions and take a fresh look at the real physiological, social, and cultural forces that make us all different. That is the focus of this section.

In Chapter 3, we will look at how differences in our brains and hormones influence each gender. In Chapter 4, we'll discuss the socialization processes that define gender behavior from birth, and how the gender messages we receive continue to influence our adult lives and work experiences. In Chapter 5, we will explore the frameworks of leading culture experts to better understand how cultural differences influence decision-making and workplace interactions.

This section is a summation in simple terms of extensive research by experts in numerous fields, including neuroscience, sociology, economics, business performance, and gender studies. It will help you manage gender and cultural differences more effectively — and open up a more honest workplace dialogue about those differences. As the experts are quick to point out, there are always exceptions and outliers — and we should not dismiss matters of personal choice, moral integrity, accountability, or individual variation. But the information we'll look at *is* a useful starting point for understanding, and learning to value, the different tendencies of gender and culture.

To use a cooking analogy, managing without understanding gender and cultural differences is like trying to make a stew without knowing the characteristics of the individual ingredients. To understand how the ingredients will blend and influence each other, and how they will contribute to the stew as a whole, we need to first appreciate them on their own.

So let's put our oft-ignored gender and culture issues "on the table" for closer examination. Male or female, and regardless of ethnic or cultural background, that's an important step in maximizing the performance and leadership potential of each individual. Looking at these "root issues" will also help you contextualize behaviors and group dynamics that may have stumped you in the past.

The information we'll cover is applicable in any country, as I've experienced firsthand in the U.S., Latin America, and Europe. A few "root issues" are more predominant in some countries than others, but I find them needing to be addressed in every engagement. I have also found that learning to identify and manage gender and culture differences is a replicable skill. In other words, the skills you develop in one setting or situation will improve your ability to deal with almost any future setting or situation you encounter.

CHAPTER 3
Physiological Differences Between Women and Men

I've worked with women in corporate settings for many years, but as I began researching this book, even I was amazed by the scientific literature addressing often overlooked differences between male and female physiology. As an increasing number of business experts and publications now recognize, failing to acknowledge and leverage those differences is a primary cause of the corporate bottleneck with regard to promoting women into positions of leadership.

As Dr. Louann Brizendine puts it in her book, *The Female Brain*: "Biology does represent the foundation of our personalities and behavioral tendencies. But if in the name of free will — and political correctness — we try to deny the influence of biology on the brain, we begin fighting our own nature."[35]

Physiological factors influence perceptions, behavior, and decision-making. If we don't factor them in, what I refer to as "poor gender communication" is inevitable. Conversely, gaining a shared understanding of these factors can do wonders to diminish conflict and improve both personal and team performance.

For example, I once went to Brazil to teach a group of executives about mentoring and coaching. Having just entered a merger with a U.S. entity, the CEO of this Brazilian company was under pressure and needed everyone on his executive team to contribute and perform to their maximum potential. He had one key resource on the transition team who was a brilliant, hard-working female — but he felt her behavior created conflict within the group.

I decided to do a role play with the CEO and this executive woman to recreate what occurred during meetings. Then we "debriefed" on what had happened by exploring all the elements from the perspective of different ways that men and women tend to perceive, think and behave. It was as if I had lifted 100 pounds off each executive's shoulders! As I saw firsthand, they interacted much more naturally and effectively after the role play — all because they'd shared a well-directed conversation that deepened their understanding of gender differences.

In this chapter, I want to focus on two key areas of physiological difference: the brain and hormones. Male and female brains and hormones *are* different — go ahead, you can say it! In fact, the differences are desirable for many reasons, including the way they predispose us to complementary interactive and leadership skills. Sadly, this subject has been "off limits" and misunderstood for so long that most people are uncomfortable even discussing it.

We have much to gain by learning our real differences and "unlearning" the rigid frames that keep us stuck. Transforming a "gender-neutral" workplace into a gender-*smart* environment can yield many organization-wide benefits:

- Leverage the full range of skills and attributes that individual men and women can contribute.
- Adapt corporate strategy, training and management processes to better fit the physiological realities of team members.
- Deflate potential conflicts among employees by using training, coaching or group dialogue to raise awareness of how gender influences behavior; replace misunderstanding with appreciation.
- Assemble more effective, higher-performing teams by balancing complementary skills and encouraging individuals to leverage what they naturally do best.
- Establish a stronger, more cohesive, better aligned culture to help managers optimize limited resources and achieve ambitious performance goals.

"Gender smart" means having a keen understanding of different skills and advantages that men and women offer, and leveraging their attributes in a strategically effective way. The bottom line is that with today's workforce, working smart *requires* being gender smart. So let's start by learning about the unique characteristics of male and female brains and hormones.

Differences Between Female and Male Brains

When I began my career in the 1970s, "male vs. female" issues were a frequent source of conflict and sometimes led to an outright impasse. Power dynamics, performance, quality of work, appropriate roles and many other topics were all tainted by stereotypes about the capabilities of men and women. The "politically correct" era that followed was in some ways worse: We still had the stereotypes, misunderstandings, and conflicts, but now we weren't even allowed to talk about them!

The big breakthrough over the past decade or so is that we now have scientific data to help us restructure the no-win "male vs. female" debate into a productive "male *and* female" dialogue. In particular, evolving brain-scan technology, including Functional MRIs and PETs, and sophisticated computer analytics have put us on firmer ground for defining physiological differences and how they impact everything from individual behavior up to macroeconomic trends.

The new research makes it clear that men and women are different — and that their different attributes, at least in the ideal situation, balance each other. Brizendine conveyed this balance in *The Female Brain* in 2006, and went on to publish a complementary volume on *The Male Brain* in 2010:

> "The female brain has tremendous, unique aptitudes — outstanding verbal agility, the capability to connect deeply in friendship, a nearly psychic capacity to read faces and tone of voice for emotions and states of mind, and the ability to defuse conflict. All of this is hardwired into the women brains. These are the natural qualities that women are born with that many men lack. Men are born with other talents shaped by their own hormonal reality."[36]

Understanding the differences between male and female brains is pertinent to developing a management approach that will accelerate performance and achieve successful outcomes. It is also critical in helping your team work better together. Everywhere I go to offer our leadership program, the responses I see in both men and women show that there is a lack of shared understanding on physiological differences and their impact. This knowledge gap gets in the way of better work environments and professional development, undermines group dynamics, and exacerbates conflicts.

Before we look at specific differences, I want to emphasize that nothing we have learned about the brain suggests that there is an overall performance difference between men and women. Rather, the research suggests that differences in how male and female brains function create a tendency for one or the other sex to be better suited to certain kinds of problem-solving or situations. I've summarized a few details from Brizendine's work in the table below. The left column shows areas of the brain that tend to be larger, more active or more sensitive in women, and the behaviors that influences. The right column does the same for the male brain.

Differences in Brain Function and Behavior

The Female Brain	The Male Brain
Anterior Cingulate Cortex — weighs options, detects conflicts and makes decisions	**Temporal Parietal Junction** — the solution seeker; during interpersonal solutions, it activates more quickly in males and looks to "fix it fast"
Insula — processes "gut feelings"	**Dorsal Premammillary Nucleus** — defend your turf, sensitivity to turf threats
Hippocampus — never forgets a fight or a tender moment	**Amygdala** — the alarm system for threats
Mirror Neuron Systems — emotional empathy, ability to feel what another feels	**Ventral Tegmental Area** — movement, motivation, reward
Prefrontal Cortex — the "CEO" of the brain; makes judgments and puts the brake on impulses	

Source: Based on tables in The Female Brain and The Male Brain
by Louann Brizendine

Here is another list of interesting differences I've summarized from Michael Gurian's book, *Leadership and the Sexes: Using Gender Science to Create Success in Business*. Again, keep in mind that there are always exceptions — these are compelling and useful averages and approximations, not absolutes:

- At any given time, there is 15% to 20% more blood flow in a woman's brain than in a man's. This helps women's brains work simultaneously in ways men's brains do not, and may explain why women tend to have a strong ability to multitask.
- The male brain enters a rest state many times during the day, whereas the female brain doesn't. This has an impact on the way women pay attention, complete tasks, relax, and talk.
- The female brain processes information and experience in different parts of the brain at different times than the male brain. This leads to different types of intelligence, and may explain the tendency for the genders to focus on different things, ideas and outcomes.
- The occipital and parietal lobes in women's brains are more active than in men's brains. This has been tied to different ways of negotiating deals, conflicts and communication processes.
- The male temporal lobe is less active than the female temporal lobe. This makes women better able to hear words and transfer what they hear, read, and see into written words.[37]

These examples just scratch the surface of the scientific research — the deeper you go, the more it becomes clear that treating male and female brains as if they are the "same" does not make sense. In some aspects, male and female brains are almost opposites, operating on different "frequencies" with different emphasis and different processes.

The good news is that knowledge is power. Knowing how physiology influences certain traits puts us in a better position to dispel misconceptions, evaluate behavior fairly, and manage individuals and teams more effectively. The functional differences of the male and female brain don't mean a resulting behavior is inevitable, nor should they become a carte blanche excuse for undesirable traits. But understanding what *is* physiological, rather than just "choice," empowers us to know how to address a situation and get the desired outcome.

One reason I wrote this book is that I see corporations missing opportunities to tap the natural synergy between male and female attributes. We can only do this effectively if we understand and value the different attributes in the first place.

For example, for physiological reasons women are predisposed to ask more questions — while men tend to want to "fix the problem fast." These natural tendencies balance each other — *if* they are understood and consciously managed. If not, they easily lead to miscommunication and frustration. Have you ever been in a meeting where a female executive seemed to ask "too many questions," and the men in the meeting became dismissive or annoyed by what they saw as unnecessary diversions?

I once coached a woman who was struggling with that problem. I first explained that, physiologically, her brain was geared to ask questions, but, physiologically, men are predisposed to take action. So one strategy was to self-regulate — to prioritize the many questions that came to her and hone in on two or three that felt most important. Other questions might better be saved for sidebar conversations with specific individuals rather than shared with the whole group.

In this strategy, the female still asks the questions she wants to ask, but sticks to specific, targeted topics that will tap the male brain's capability for bursts of focused attention. The goal is to play to the strengths of each gender, so that the meeting will feel congruent to both.

After a couple sessions, this woman's supervisor told me she had become a completely different person! Well, it wasn't her innate desire to ask questions that changed, nor the value of her questions — what changed was that she learned to channel her natural quality to work more effectively with the natural qualities of her male colleagues.

The same lesson is just as important in reverse. If you have a female on your team who males are tuning out because she asks "too many questions" or "is too emotionally intense," it's critical for you to remind the men that cascading questions can greatly enhance decision-making. They need to self-regulate their tendency to shut questions down, appreciate that there is value in how the female brain works, and embrace a shared process that integrates everyone's strengths.

Remember our "Lehman Brothers and Sisters" section earlier? Research done after the 2008 financial meltdown showed that a lack of critical questions and a tendency by primarily male decision-makers to dismiss challenges were root causes of the problem. Here are a few quick pointers to help you avoid that scenario and tap the complementary strengths of the male *and* female brains on your team:

- Coach women on effective communication (e.g., encourage a focus on targeted communication and top-value questions).
- Help male team members understand that questioning is natural for female team members — and valuable for the whole team. Reassure them that although they may feel that a woman is "too intense" or is creating more work or threatening their views, the reality is that she is just contributing in a mode that is slightly different from theirs.
- Coach men on good listening skills; encourage them to be patient, and to actively engage with the person posing the question.
- Lead by example. Be a bridge. In group settings, we take our cues from the lead manager. If he or she says, "wait, let's stop and address that question," it will signify everyone to deepen their attention.

How Hormones Shape Female *and* Male Behavior

Due to advances in technology, we now understand just how much hormones influence behaviors and decision-making — in both genders and at all ages. As Brizendine tells us, "Hormones can determine what the brain is interested in doing….They can affect being rough-and-tumble, competing in sports…solving problems, interpreting facial expressions and other's emotions" and much more.[38]

Understanding the impact of hormones is important in managing individual and group performance, yet no subject has been more taboo for corporate professionals — as I have experienced firsthand. To give you one example, my firm was once asked to launch a women's leadership initiative at a Wall Street law firm. As part of that initiative we did a training session with a group of female lawyers. All had excellent credentials, but said they felt stuck — like they had done everything right but had not been rewarded with a partnership position.

As we began talking about the importance of physiological differences and the impact of hormones on behavior, the women almost revolted! They were insulted that we would mention hormones in the context of a women's leadership program. Immersed in a male-dominated law environment, they found the idea of exploring traits that differentiate women unacceptable, irrelevant, perhaps even painful.

This is not uncommon. Professional women often spend so much time thinking, behaving, and reacting to clients and peers in a genderless or male-emulating way that they lose their ability to relate to the most significant attributes that would make them a strategic treasure for their organization.

Neither women nor managers and corporations can afford to continue ignoring the reality that physiological differences are part of what stimulates behavior and, in some cases, creates conflict. Let's explore some of the research in this area — looking first at men, then at women. We'll close this chapter with a section reviewing the sum of male and female physiological differences — and why balancing gender can lead to better performance and decision-making.

Male Hormones

There has been increased discussion recently about the influence of male hormones on decision-making, but the topic is not new. For example, back in 1990, Dr. Robert Rose, now at the University of Texas Medical Branch, was performing research that led him to tie hormones to a propensity for certain behaviors, including linking testosterone to increased competitiveness and dominance.

Testosterone levels are generally 10 to 20 times higher in men than women, and even the highest levels measured in women usually fall in the low range for men. Various studies over the years have linked this to real differences in behavior and decision-making. For example, the interaction of testosterone and vasopressin is known to trigger aggression, the need to occupy space, and a desire for control. On the positive side, that can make men more decisive, quick to take action, and inclined to lead the way. On the negative side, it can also cause men to make hasty decisions, underrate the impact of immediate conflicts on larger goals, and become overly domineering.

More recent contributions to this field include the work of Dr. John Coates, a former Wall Street trader who is now a neuroscientist at Cambridge University. In 2008, Coates and Cambridge colleague Joe Herbert published the results of a study in which they measured the levels of testosterone and cortisol in male stock traders over the course of the business day. Among other findings, they concluded that:

> "a trader's morning testosterone level predicts his day's prof-itability. We also found that a trader's cortisol rises with both the variance of his trading results and the volatility of the market....Our results point to a further possibility: tes-tosterone and cortisol are known to have cognitive and behavioral effects, so if the acutely elevated steroids we observed were to persist or increase as volatility rises, they may shift risk preferences and even affect a trader's ability to engage in rational choice."[39]

This suggests an interesting scenario. With elevated testosterone levels boosting confidence, traders might be comfortable taking larger risks which can lead to bigger returns. But the same testosterone "rush" could also impact their ability to gauge risk factors. If the market, or individual trades, underperform, the hormonal balance then shifts toward cortisol, the "fight or flight" hormone which can be triggered by uncertainty. The hormonal cocktail could further compromise judgment.

Keeping in mind that stock trading is a predominantly male profession, it's not unreasonable to wonder whether hormones play a role in the higher highs of market "bubbles" and the lower lows of big sell-offs. In fact, Coates looks at the behavior of the financial markets during 2008 and 2009 in just this light in a new book titled *The Hour Between Dog and Wolf: Risk Taking, Gut Feelings and the Biology of Boom and Bust*. In addition to exploring the ups and downs of testosterone and cortisol, he also talks about the vagus nerve. When functioning well, the vagus nerve enables heart rate and adrenalin levels to rise quickly in a crisis, then quickly return to normal. But constant exposure to the testosterone-cortisol roller-coaster can impair the nerve, leaving a person in a constantly "stressed" state. Coates concludes that better gender and generational balance in the trading profession would likely mean fewer market dramas.[40]

All of this may be new to you — and perhaps sound a bit radical. In terms of workforce and leadership issues, the only hormones most people think about are female hormones associated with mood swings, as if women alone are plagued by these powerful chemicals. Men have been neglected in this conversation, but the research makes it clear that they too have hormonal mood swings and behavioral shifts that impact both their personal lives and business performance.

Female Hormones

Female hormones have historically received more attention than male hormones, but the attention tends to be oversimplified. Understanding the more complex truth of female hormones — including higher levels of estrogen, progesterone, serotonin, and oxytocin than men — is important to help frame behavior that males might consider "too emotional." In particular, studies show that the interaction between estrogen and oxytocin predisposes women toward the following characteristics:

- More verbal, including a tendency to ask more questions and be inquisitive
- More empathetic, with a strong desire to "bond" with colleagues, especially other females
- More collaborative, inclusive; the "we" factor
- More willing to share power and success; tend to seek and create egalitarian environments

It is also good to be aware that women undergo intense hormonal changes over the course of their lives, especially those who go through pregnancy. Behavioral tendencies (and benefits) change at different stages. In a woman's 20s and 30s, intense daily changes in estrogen, progesterone and testosterone can lead to a high level of emotional awareness and control, and a corresponding sense of balance and maturity in decision-making. During pregnancy, increases in progesterone and estrogen tend to make women calmer. As women enter their 40s and 50s, lower levels of estrogen and lack of progesterone, often combined with diminishing roles as caretakers, can inspire a different balance that is more driven and focused. In fact, I recommend paying special attention to female Baby Boomers. These women are often ready to reinvent themselves and redefine their contribution as professionals — and potential senior leaders.

Balancing the Equation

In a world where most leadership teams are "male only" or predominantly male, it makes sense to think about how women's "natural programming" can provide a desirable balance for your team and the organization as a whole. To cite two examples from the previous section, whereas testosterone can sometimes cause too much focus on individual performance, women are more likely to see the "big picture" and consider collective goals. Likewise, the male tendency to want to take action quickly is balanced by the female tendency to slow down and consider multiple ideas. Keeping this knowledge in front of you can help you understand recurring "gender frustration" scenarios and hopefully transform them into "gender appreciation" and performance-boosting balance.

To be sure, such balance will not happen overnight. It will require conscientious effort from both sides, but especially men, since their normal mindset is to associate action with leadership. At the same time, this is no call for paralysis by analysis. In seeking balance, the male "take action" energy can be just as important to keep a process moving as the female "consideration" energy can be as a needed brake. The point is that once we make balance the goal, we can better identify and address the deep-rooted misconceptions that stand in our way and often lead to male-female conflict.

The physiological differences we've touched on in this chapter are science — not stereotype. We will all be less conflicted and more productive if we accept that these differences, along with the socialization differences we'll explore in the next chapter, result in different behavioral tendencies. Let me summarize some that I think are particularly relevant in a business context:

Gender Tendencies

Females Are More Likely to...	Males Are More Likely to...
Seek collaboration and build connections	Gravitate toward hierarchical structure; want to assert themselves as the leader or have a clear idea of where they fit in "the pecking order"
Perceive and work toward collective goals; use "we" when talking about performance	Focus on maximizing individual performance
Want to ask questions and weigh a range of variables before making a decision	Want to take decisive action quickly; more linear, direct "fix it fast" approach
Attuned to subtle changes or distinctions in vocal tone, facial expression and body language; good at "reading between the lines"	Minimize social and personal data; less inclined to seek out or facilitate social interactions in general
Experience and express empathy; easily put themselves in other people's shoes	Emphasize results specific to themselves or their team without worrying about broader consequences or impact on others
Develop and apply emotional intelligence	Downplay emotional expression
Want to prevent conflict and find conciliatory outcomes, which can lead to internal stress	Depersonalize conflict, allowing them to navigate disagreements more easily, but also sometimes fail to address the "real" problem
Look for (and respond to) outward signs of approval or disapproval	Promote themselves; less concerned with how others feel
Mirror behavior of others and adapt to be complementary; develop a deep resonance with people they know for a long time that allows them to predict behavior	Develop a sense of tactical independence

Awareness of these tendencies can help you understand and develop individuals more effectively, assemble teams strategically to balance desirable qualities, and ensure less gender-conflicted communication and interaction among those you manage.

Providing a more accurate, complete and science-based framework for men and women to understand each other helps dispel misconceptions and remove barriers to effective collaboration. Instead of resenting or trying to change a man's individualistic focus or a woman's empathy, we can start from the premise that both are, in large part, "built in" qualities that can be equally valuable depending on the situation. Instead of resigning ourselves to an adversarial "Venus vs. Mars" relationship, we can work toward a more inclusive environment where differences are seen as complementary and leveraged in smarter, more strategic ways.

This reframing has proven especially transformative in the work I do to help corporations develop female talent and improve overall business performance. When men and women see each other more clearly, and feel more comfortable being themselves, there are many benefits:

- Women's careers accelerate. Women get more promotions and stretch assignments which offer rich opportunities for strategic thinking and leadership development.
- Women feel empowered because they are encouraged to build on authentic strengths.
- Understanding the physiological dynamics behind behavior, men and women have less negative, less personal reactions to differences. This leads to more collegial, synergistic interactions that focus on finding the best way to accomplish objectives.
- Communication improves. There is less anxiety about gender-based misunderstandings. Women don't feel "invisible" or "unheard."
- Knowing that their differences are respected, women are more willing and able to contribute, even in predominantly male environments.
- Both genders are freed from the energy-draining need to "walk on eggshells" or suppress differences.

Our chemical makeup prompts different and complementary behaviors — and a growing body of research, as well as my own experiences, show that companies and even whole countries perform better when there is a conscious effort to bring these differences into balance. To go back to our "Lehman Brothers and Sisters" example, how different would the outcome have been if the male need to take action quickly had been balanced by the female need to "ask more questions" and weigh a broader range of variables?

The more I travel through Europe, Latin America and the U.S., the more convinced I am that understanding and balancing gender and cultural differences will separate the new economy's high performers from those struggling just to survive.

The first step to being one of those high performers is committing yourself and your company to learning what science can teach us about gender differences, and unlearning old assumptions that have held men and women back from achieving their potential as individuals and together. Today could be the start of a new path that will be good for your career, good for your company, and more fulfilling for everyone — enjoy!

CHAPTER 4
Socialization Differences Between Women and Men

We've seen that physiological differences predispose women and men toward different behaviors, but gender is also shaped (some even argue that it is primarily "constructed") by how most girls and boys are raised and socialized. Society imprints gender-specific roles and expectations on us that continue impacting us when we reach adulthood and enter a business environment. If not examined carefully, these roles and expectations can make it difficult for women and men to interact effectively and develop congruent work relationships.

As with physiological differences, it can be challenging to get people to think about and discuss socialization due to our "don't ask, don't tell" approach to gender. When my firm does consulting and training, we often encounter resistance from both women and men if we suggest that communication dilemmas or workforce problems are rooted, in part, in the way we were raised.

That resistance tends to be stronger among younger people who feel that socialization differences may have been significant in the past, but now we have a more egalitarian culture where girls and boys compete in the same sports and are exposed to the same opportunities. It's true that there has been progress in some respects, but most of our *fundamental* gender messaging remains much the same as it's been for decades, or potentially even more conflicting. Caitlin Flanagan's *Girl Land*, for example, examines the impact of social media on girls' socialization, describing how this world of constant connectivity, message exchange, and emotional intensity further elevates popularity and being liked over attributes like intellectual development and self-discovery.[41]

The bottom line, to reiterate a key point of this book, is that managing men and women *fairly* and *effectively* does not mean managing everyone in exactly the same way. It is critical to understand that men and women come from different places and therefore respond differently, are motivated differently, and have different strengths to develop.

I will also emphasize that the ideas in this chapter are not simply a matter of personal opinion. Most come from expert sources and have been used by numerous other writers exploring the impact of gender. Where appropriate, I quote these sources directly so you can look up the original material if you wish to learn more. The value of what I've done in this chapter is to combine such ideas *with* my personal observations and insights in the specific context of managing women in the workforce, developing leadership skills, and improving overall performance.

The Blue and the Pink: Making "The Invisible Shield" Visible

From the moment we are born, parents and society project gender-based traits and expectations that will shape our identity and our sense of where we fit into the world around us. Baby boys and girls are treated differently, communicated to differently, described differently, and given encouragement (or discouragement) for different behaviors. It's blue for baby boys and pink for baby girls.

That pinkness or blueness creates what I call "the invisible shield" — a structure between us and the world that colors our perceptions and others' perceptions of us. This is not all bad. However, the "shield" can become a "cage" for many people, constraining growth or making them feel excluded in certain social contexts. There are many examples of this when we look at what holds women back from senior leadership. The "shield" can also become a barrier that prevents men and women from communicating clearly and working together more effectively.

In a sense, the problems come from the shield's "invisibility" more than its pinkness or blueness. If we don't *see* this layer of socialization impacting our perceptions and behaviors, we can't learn how to understand it, or adapt it in different circumstances. To move our shields, use them effectively, or drop them altogether when appropriate, we must first acknowledge that we're holding them.

Let's try to make the invisible shield more visible — and movable — by exploring some basic socialization messages that tend to separate men and women and create challenges when we try to collaborate.

As babies and infants, girls tend to be treated more gently, as if they are more fragile, weaker, and in need of greater protection than baby boys. They are held with care and spoken to in tones that are soft, low in pitch, melodious, and loving. With boys, there is less touching in general, and the tone of voice tends to be more forceful and direct. In many societies there are also real valuation differences right from the start. In the most extreme examples, such as India and China, girls are deemed less desirable and pegged to a secondary status. But even in countries like the U.S., it is not uncommon to hear about families "hoping for a boy."

In pre-school and grade school, the differences rise another notch. Research has shown that boys tend to get more physical and verbal rewards than girls, and more individual instruction on how to do things. They get more praise, especially when they win, are assertive, or behave as if they are in control. Girls get almost the exact opposite message — they are discouraged from being "too competitive," "bossy" or "not nice" even in situations where they excel. Boys are expected to be tough, and are taught to respond to pain or difficulty with minimal emotion — setting the stage for adult males to act detached or indifferent even in highly emotional contexts. Young girls on the other hand are expected to be emotional — and may even find that over-emoting draws more attention than achievement.

The early years also start one of the most significant areas of difference that impact later workforce dynamics: "speaking up." Whether at home, in school, or elsewhere, boys are not only "allowed" to make spontaneous comments, it is encouraged as a sign of leadership and assertiveness. In contrast, girls are discouraged or even punished for calling out without permission. From an early age, girls learn to wait their turn to speak while boys are taught to do the opposite. Is it any surprise that later men will have no problem "speaking their minds" in business meetings while women often miss opportunities to contribute and say they feel "unheard"?

The "encouragement gap" continues in high school, particularly in traditionally "male" subjects like math. As Anna Fels points out in her book *Necessary Dreams*, "girls and boys enter high school with similar math achievement, but by senior year boys outperform girls in every math category." The explanation? Fels cites a study of teacher responses to students in high school math classes where researchers found that "girls received only 30% of encouraging comments but 84% of discouraging comments."[42]

Muriel Niederle and Lise Vesterlund, economics professors at Stanford and the University of Pittsburgh respectively, came to a similar conclusion in their research on the gender gap in math test scores. Among other interesting observations, they explain that "the strong stereotype of male superior math performance may influence the confidence of females and affect their performance." Looking at how the gender gap plays out at the college level, they cite a report on the responses of women who dropped out of math-intensive college majors. In most cases, decisions were driven not by skills but by "women negatively interpreting their grades and having low self-confidence" or by "negative aspects of their schools' climate, such as competition, lack of support, and discouraging faculty and peers."[43]

I can almost guarantee that "the invisible shield" is creating challenges for women and men in your workforce. We can't give men and women such divergent messages about "acceptable" behavior, expectations and self-esteem for most of two decades, and then suddenly demand congruent behavior when they enter the workplace.

The Imprint of "Play" on How We Interact

Much research has explored how early gender preferences for toys or games has a long-term impact on men and women. Additionally, in many cultures, girls play almost exclusively with girls, and boys play with boys. In the U.S., girls who are interested in boy's games and play with boys have historically been known as "tomboys." The stigma of crossing the gender line has lessened somewhat for individual children, but looking at group dynamics in general, and workforce issues specifically, we see that gender-based "play" roles continue to strongly influence later interactions.

Differences in the types of games most boys and girls play also remain noteworthy. In general, boys are directed toward games such as soccer, football, or baseball. Playing these sports builds fundamental skills that are valued in corporate culture: competitiveness, an embrace of challenges and conflicts, a desire to win, a focus on performance, teamwork, the ability to "depersonalize" failure, and so on.

Conversely, girls are often encouraged to pursue less directly competitive activities such as ballet. But even in sports like soccer or basketball, where their participation is on the rise, they are expected to "play nice" and avoid fighting and conflict. The "social voice" they hear tells them it's better to share, to give up power to keep friends happy — to essentially prioritize relational factors over winning or personal performance. From an early age, this "play" framework effectively tells girls that their presence and value depends on being liked — while boys are taught to define themselves by individual performance, toughness, and even "conquering."

Legislation such as Title IX in the U.S. may help even out the number of girls and boys who participate in sports, but the takeaways continue to be very different. For girls, competition is still a risky proposition that may invite criticism or ostracization. For boys, it is central and celebrated — even among friends, the real joy and sense of self comes not from "playing together" but from claiming victory over the opponent.

It's not hard to see how this plays out later in life. Boys well-schooled in competing become men who hold their ground and have a natural instinct to look for one-up opportunities that help them "win." They see disagreements at work as part of the normal give-and-take of struggling for position and power, nothing personal. Girls, given the legacy of needing to "play nice" and avoid conflict at all costs, cede opportunities, relinquish power and strive for harmony even when it's not in their best interests.

I have seen these dynamics thwart performance in numerous situations. Women shy away from claiming their place in meetings, negotiating for better work and compensation, asking for the power to hire and fire, and so on. Men assume that women are too passive, too conflict-adverse to hold their ground or lead.

At most companies, resolving such situations will fall on a manager like you. Keep in mind that this isn't just an interpersonal issue — these gender gaps can undermine a team's alignment and jeopardize its ability to move forward and achieve its goals. Don't wait for someone to come storming into your office with a gender-related complaint. Be alert to subtle signs that interactions could be going awry and take action to ensure that otherwise talented professionals don't become "trapped" by socialized gender roles.

The men on your team will be inclined to compete and protect their position. The women on your team may tend to not speak up if they feel it will create conflict. To help bridge the gap, take such differences into account and:

- Coach communication; teach women that it's important to be assertive, and that sometimes conflict can be productive
- Pay attention to group dynamics, particularly if your team has more men than women; if you notice a lack of female participation, reach out and request input
- Make it clear to men that "winning" means working as a team, and you can't afford to have anyone shut down a valuable suggestion or team member just to protect personal turf
- Proactively manage discussions to ensure that all viewpoints are considered and reach out to individuals who may be wrestling with conflicts between how they were socialized and how they can best advance their careers and contribute to the team

I'll add one more point — which is also a good lead-in to the next chapter. Culture is critical. The truth is that almost all corporate cultures are based on a male paradigm. If the game is set up to favor male strengths, is it any wonder that you're having a hard time retaining talented women and moving them into positions of leadership? It may be helpful to think about how you can change your culture to facilitate more gender-balanced teams and leadership. For example, is your corporate culture one that rewards people for being aggressive and taking a "no holds barred" approach to personal success? Do management or promotion processes tend to set up subordinates to compete against each other? Is the "one up" attitude celebrated even if it means other people feel shut down?

"That's just how we do things" is no longer a good answer. We need to ask how we *should* do things in order to help all individuals realize their full potential — and drive the company to realize *its* full potential.

CHAPTER 5
Identifying and Understanding the Impact of Culture Differences

So far in Section II, I've focused mostly on gender, but my work, and this book, are really about leveraging gender *and* culture differences to drive better business performance.

In my earliest consulting work doing business development for multinational corporations, I became aware of how critical gender and culture differences were to closing deals and ensuring long-term success. I also learned about certain frameworks and strategies that were very effective in bridging those differences. As I transitioned from business development to my current work in leadership training, I began formally collecting these materials and presenting them to clients.

There are many parallels between gender and culture. In fact, aspects of socialization discussed in Chapter 4 are essentially the cultural norms that shape gender. In both gender and culture, our fundamental challenge is to embrace differences — which means giving up on the assimilationist approach of asking employees to shed their differences and "blend in."

It also means that your diversity strategy must ascend beyond quotas and tokenism, which research consistently shows just undermine performance and erode confidence in top management. Moving toward the goal of true integration, where authentic differences are appreciated and merit-based opportunities are presented fairly, is not only good for individuals, it is good for business.

You may begin that journey over a specific issue, like improving the presence of women in your leadership pipeline or making adjustments to more effectively manage the workforce in a new country where your company is expanding operations. But the good news is that once you learn to understand and leverage differences for one group, you will find the same lessons and strategies highly effective for others as well.

Before we explore two top-level frameworks that can help you better understand cultural differences, let's start by looking at what we mean by "culture" in the first place. Merriam-Webster defines culture as:

> "**a:** the integrated pattern of human behavior that includes thought, speech, action, and artifacts and depends upon the human capacity for learning and transmitting knowledge to succeeding generations; **b:** the customary beliefs, social forms, and material traits of a racial, religious, or social group; **c:** the set of shared attitudes, values, goals, and practices that characterizes an institution or organization; **d:** the set of values, conventions, or social practices associated with a particular field, activity, or societal characteristic"[44]

This definition tells us two important things. First, "culture" can come from many directions — not just ethnicity, race, or nationality, but subtle sources like your profession. Indeed, in the global economy, most of us are truly a product of multiple cultures. That includes "corporate culture." The norms promoted, expected or enforced throughout a company can impact individuals (for good or ill) as much as any other form of culture.

A second characteristic of "culture" in this definition is that it has both depth and breadth — we are talking about the entire range of beliefs, values, assumptions, and practices that make us who we are, shape our self-image and perceptions, define our relationships, set up power dynamics, and so on. In that sense, culture is a dominant component of our behavioral DNA.

To understand and overcome challenges related to managing a diverse workforce, we have to be able and willing to dissect that DNA — in ourselves as well as the "other." In fact, a first step we take with many of our clients involves "culture shock" exercises designed to wake participants to just how much we are all influenced by our culture — and how much we rely on stereotypes regarding those outside our comfort zone of "people like us."

These exercises help open a dialogue that in many corporations has been considered "out of bounds." Many HR directors I work with confess that their approach and the resulting "corporate message" are part of the problem. Since they tend to be compliance-focused, they are often attached to a version of "equality" that requires sameness — which leaves little room to develop practices more organically or factor in the real differences that are inevitable with a diverse workforce.

Laws and rules have their place, but they alone will never get us to the goal of a high-performing workplace where individuals feel they can achieve their full potential. If anything, humans find "have to" behavior constraining and demotivating — even when they agree with the principles behind a rule. Instead, we need to promote greater self-awareness combined with better understanding of our place in a bigger picture — a state that I sometimes call "unique-globalness."

Understanding the attributes and experiences that make each of us unique is a prerequisite for understanding how we are interrelated — and how best to manage and reframe our responses to the other gender or those from other cultures. While I do this work as a business consultant, I will add that it is also meaningful for me personally and often life-changing for participants. For many, it is the first time they have been free to talk about gender and culture differences in an honest way.

Culture is an enormous topic, but in the context of *Can You Afford to Ignore Me?* I want to hone in on a few "structural tools" I use with my clients. Based on the work of two leading experts who have spent their professional lives studying cultural differences, these tools are not specific to any one culture; instead, they provide top-level frameworks that can improve our understanding and interaction with *any* culture.

Each researcher has looked at culture from a different angle. Edward Hall, an anthropologist, was primarily interested in how culture impacts verbal and nonverbal communication. Geert Hofstede, a social psychologist, has done intensive research in a number of areas, including how people acquire culture and how that process and the values conveyed influence behavior in a given social structure. He has also applied his insights to the influence of organizational culture on business.

Framework 1: Edward Hall's High Context - Low Context[45]

Different cultures may have very different communication styles. A grasp of basic communication principles is critical to understanding those from other cultures — and making sure you are understood *by* them. One of the most powerful tools in this regard is Edward Hall's theory of high-context and low-context cultures, published in his bestseller *Beyond Culture*.

High-context cultures emphasize personal relationships, the collective good, and the value of group harmony and consensus. In Japan, a high-context culture, there is a popular saying that "the nail that stands out gets banged down." To be humble is a good quality, and self-promotion is frowned upon. It is expected that an individual will share successful outcomes and put group achievement ahead of personal performance. The notion of individual performance itself is blurred — in a sense, it is indistinguishable from collective performance.

That's very different from a low-context culture like the U.S. where individual performance has a central role in our perceptions and communication style. Companies in low-context cultures tend to create a dual scenario — while teamwork is valued in many situations, every individual is evaluated separately. A certain amount of ego is not only acceptable, it's vital. The nail that *doesn't* stand out may be seen as not contributing enough or unworthy of promotion.

If you have high-context team members working in a low-context corporate culture, this presents a challenge. As a manager, you have to be careful to distinguish between differences in performance among team members and differences in their ability to *promote* performance. You might need to coach high-context team members to adapt their definition of achievement, express themselves more assertively, and understand the value of personal ambition in your environment. In their cultures, after all, the "right" thing to do is diminish individual performance and defer to a collective effort.

Developing trust is a key factor in communicating well within a high-context culture. Simpatico is important — people need to be comfortable with you and like you. First impressions are critical, but a high-context individual may also require time to make sure interacting with you "feels right." If you're from a low-context culture, you may find this process too subjective — or too personal.

The scope of communication also tends to be more complex in a high-context culture. Specific words, or even facts, are only part of the puzzle. Someone from a high-context culture pays close attention to tone of voice, facial expression, body language, the speaker's background and status, and so on. To communicate effectively with someone from such a culture, you need to be sensitive to this and ready to read between the lines. Sometimes what is not said will be as important as what is.

Communications between peers and superiors in high-context cultures tend to be formal and structured. Low-context environments are more informal — there may be a measured degree of deference to authority, but there is a deeper assumption that "we are all equal." It is common to refer to people by first name and treat them the same regardless of position or experience.

Another characteristic of high-context communication is that it tends to be less direct. Team members from a high-context culture may find it especially hard to articulate anything that might be perceived as "bad news" or lead to conflict. As a manager, you may need to more actively solicit their input and reassure them that pointing out certain mistakes or flaws is seen as a way to *help* the team.

In low-context cultures, communication is more direct and concise. Logic and facts are valued more than intuition or the layers of personal information that influence the meaning of high-context communications. For low-context individuals, workplace communications are all about efficiency and taking action. Driven by the "time is money" dictum, the goal is to collect facts, analyze options, and make a decision as quickly as possible. Companies in low-context cultures typically structure meetings around point-by-point agendas that conclude with action plans and next steps.

Hall's framework illuminates some fundamental differences between two types of culture that need to be bridged for effective cross-cultural communication. As a manager, understanding the context your employees communicate from is the first step toward coaching them effectively in how to communicate with each other, and assisting in their professional development. It can also help you make assignments, assemble teams and establish processes that fit the communication strengths and expectations of different individuals while avoiding potential communication gaps.

Many of my clients have been companies from low-context cultures who need to reframe expectations, communication style, and even business behaviors in order to succeed in high-context markets. Whether it involves members of the workforce, suppliers, or potential customers, I emphasize that making the journey from low context to high context requires patience.

You must invest more time researching backgrounds and building relationships, and you may need to slow down and explain certain processes or decisions that you take for granted in your own culture.

Similarly, I coach many managers and executives from high-context cultures as they are trying to adapt to working for a low-context employer. Here a key point is that efficient decision-making and swift execution are highly valued, so performing well may require them to "try on" behaviors that they initially worry are "too quick to action," too aggressive, or likely to cause conflict.

Doing the "pre-work" of trying to understand each other's cultures and taking proactive steps to adapt accordingly is well worth the effort. When we take the time to build a good bridge *between* high-context and low-context cultures, or between other culture types we'll look at next, relationships evolve with more ease, conflicts and misunderstandings are reduced, and we enhance our chances of unifying to achieve peak performance.

Framework Two: Geert Hofstede's Six Dimensions of Culture[46]

Another valuable framework in navigating cultural differences comes from Geert Hofstede, an engineer who held professional and managerial positions in several industrial settings before earning a PhD in Social Psychology and pioneering the study of organizational culture. His work with IBM International led to the creation of an enormous database of more than 100,000 employee surveys from 70 different countries. Based on years of analyzing this and related data, he ultimately identified four comparative dimensions to define the cultural forces that guide most individual behavior.

Subsequent research by him and, most recently, Gert Jan Hofstede and Michael Minkov, have added two more dimensions to the original model. Looking at these dimensions, and thinking about where we fall and where team members fall, generates excellent insights about both individual and collective decision-making and behavior. I highly recommend both the book that this section's material is drawn from, *Cultures and Organizations: Software of the Mind, 3rd Revised Edition*, and Professor Hofstede's *Culture's Consequences: Comparing Values, Behaviors, Institutions and Organizations Across Nations*.

Masculinity and Femininity

I've talked about cultural aspects of gender throughout this book — but one of Hofstede's insights is to look at gender as a characteristic that defines a culture. In a feminine culture, values are more homogeneous, care is central, and there is a tendency toward collaborative behavior. In a masculine culture, there is more variation in values generally, and a larger gap may exist between male and female norms. In a highly masculine society, men tend to be competitive, assertive and have the last word. Since we deal with gender differences thoroughly throughout this book, I won't go into further detail about this dimension in this section. Let's move on to dimensions that may be less familiar to you.

Large Power Distance and Small Power Distance

Hofstede's Power Distance Index (PDI) gauges how people in a society perceive and give power to others. When the PDI is small, there is broader access to power and even people not in power see it as attainable. This tends to encourage more independent thinking and individual assertiveness. A large power distance means that power is concentrated and inequality is a fact of life — people generally accept that there is a hierarchy, and only a few get to make important decisions and control outcomes. An employee from such a culture may therefore feel uncomfortable making critical decisions by themselves — they want direction and guidance.

I had a situation exemplifying this challenge while consulting for a U.S.-headquartered pharmaceutical company. I was managing a group of young professionals from Latin America, and we all reported to a senior leader based in Miami. During every conference call, the group would ask for specific action guides from the U.S. leader. His response was always something like, "Well, what do you think?" or "What would you do?"

Being from a small power distance culture, he was doing his best to democratize decision-making and encourage personal participation. However, since he was dealing with professionals from a large power distance culture, this approach was ineffective. After each meeting, I would get bombarded by follow-up calls from team members. In essence, one of my roles became to bridge the gap between a small power distance leader and large power distance team so they knew what to do. Unfortunately, the leader's inability to speak his team's "power distance language" also impacted how they viewed him. Team members would say things to me like, "This guy doesn't seem to know much — he can't even decide what he wants us to do!"

While small power distance aligns with the trend toward "flat" or "horizontal" management structures and decentralized decision-making, remember that there are still many places in the world where employees want, and even need, a more structured, authoritarian approach.

The challenge happens in reverse as well. Managers in more hierarchical corporate cultures can find it difficult to satisfy and motivate small power distance professionals who expect to have a role in decision-making and need to feel a high degree of ownership in their work process. Such individuals may be quick to challenge authority, particularly if they feel it's for the good of a project. They don't recognize authority based on position or title — and may lash out against authority that they don't feel has merit or competency.

Individualism and Collectivism

In what Hofstede calls individualistic societies, people are expected to take care only of themselves and immediate family. People see life in the context of the "I" — their own efforts, abilities, and success. In contrast, people in collective societies feel a high degree of connection with extended family and other social groups. The "we" takes precedence over the "I" — loyalty and keeping social networks strong and integrated define quality of life. In the most collectivist cultures, the "I" may even be perceived as something to censor. People in such societies find it difficult to say "no" in many situations, particularly if an authority figure is involved.

A good illustration of this — and a tragic one — was the unusually high number of plane crashes experienced by Korean Air during the 1990s. In examining the causes of these accidents, it was determined that crew co-pilots had a "paralyzing" mental framework when it came to challenging authority. That's not surprising given that Korea is a collectivist, large power distance culture where hierarchy is very important and the "I" is expected to defer to authority figures. But it became problematic in the cockpit of complex airplanes designed to have two people paying full attention to everything. Essentially what was happening was that when a pilot made a mistake, the co-pilot wouldn't feel it was his "place" to correct him! The good news is that once Korean Air identified the problem, they were able to address it.

That's a good lesson for managers. When you have individuals from more collectivist cultures, be alert to the possibility that even a highly talented professional may remain silent about problems due to their cultural "programming." To ensure top performance, you will need to take steps to actively engage such team members and give them express authority to participate and disagree with you or others.

Uncertainty: High Tolerance and Low Tolerance

Hofstede's Uncertainty Avoidance Index (UAI) helps us pay attention to another interesting difference in cultures: the ability to tolerate uncertainty. Cultures with a low tolerance for the unknown have a strong UAI — they create rigid structures and strict rules, value predictability, and tend to perceive the world in black and white. Societies that have a weak UAI are more comfortable tolerating gray areas and ambiguity. As a result, the attitude is more lax and there is less need for precise rules and laws.

There are some logical ways this plays out in terms of corporate culture. For example, in a company whose success depends on innovation and creativity, it may be important to have a weak UAI culture that encourages individuals to experiment. On the other hand, in certain manufacturing environments where precision and high quality are essential and safety is a life-or-death matter, it makes sense that you'd want a strong UAI culture. Your hiring practices should be mindful of these realities.

Long-Term Orientation and Short-Term Orientation

Obvious differences probably come to mind when you think about long-term and short-term orientations, but Hofstede's work shows how these orientations can manifest in a range of personal qualities and behaviors. In a society with a short-term orientation, for example, he finds a belief in absolute Truth, great respect for tradition, adherence to established norms, and a focus on quick results. In cultures with a long-term orientation, "truth" is seen as situational, adaptability is highly valued, and there is a focus on investing and persevering to achieve future goals.

In corporate settings, a person with a long-term orientation may be better for ongoing projects that could evolve and present new challenges along the way. Someone with a short-term orientation will be more likely to have the "time is money" mindset, and can provide value in projects where quick decisions and swift implementation are desired.

In reality, of course, the situation is rarely that simple. As a manager, you will likely have team members at various places on the long-term/short-term spectrum. Optimal outcomes will depend on anticipating and addressing challenges and finding an appropriate balance. For example, when you work with someone who has a short-term orientation, you may need to balance their natural urgency to act with reminders about due diligence. Conversely, someone with a long-term orientation may need support to help them understand the need to adhere to certain processes and deadlines.

In my own experience, I've found that it is also important to realize that people from different orientations may assign different meaning or emphasis to the same phrases. For example, "we expect to have a decision tomorrow" will be taken very literally by people from a short-term orientation culture, but for those in a long-term orientation culture, the meaning may be more like "we are very close to making a decision."

Differences in work style should also be considered. People with a long-term orientation tend to feel a need to have more than one or two people involved in decision-making, and it is not unusual for them to add stakeholders or influencers to a project or process at midstream. If short-term team members are not prepared for that, they will find it frustrating and inefficient, and it could cause conflict. The same will be true for long-term team members who aren't prepared for the quicker decision-making and "by the book" approach of short-term colleagues. Your value as a manager is to bridge these differences and help everyone understand when and why it is appropriate for different orientations to take priority in a given situation.

Indulgence and Restraint

The most recent addition to Hofstede's framework looks at the issue of gratification. In an indulgent culture, gratification of basic desires is not only permitted, it is often celebrated. Phrases like "you should do what you want" and "follow your passion" are common currency, and there may be a natural resistance to rules, processes, or authority figures who restrict the "pursuit of happiness." In a culture that leans toward the restraint side of this dimension, personal gratification may be seen as selfish, damaging to community or group values, or even immoral. In a culture of restraint, people tend to value traditions and rules.

This dimension is fairly new, so ideas on how it applies to managing a diverse workforce are still evolving. Countries in North America, Latin America, and parts of Africa tend to have indulgent cultures, while Asian and Muslim countries tend to have cultures of restraint. In my experience, the most significant aspect of this dimension may be a team member's feelings about authority. If you're trying to manage and motivate someone from an indulgent culture, you need to emphasize their personal participation and the positive rewards of a project. Dictating demands and "thou shalt nots" will not be effective. Conversely, a team member from a culture of restraint may have a hard time with a project or work environment that feels too "loose" and lacks clear rules and lines of authority.

Applying the Tools

This chapter is only a starting point — many books have been written about the frameworks I've just summarized. But I hope the overview has awakened you to the complex forces behind cultural differences — and the wide range of assumptions and behaviors you will encounter in our increasingly global workforce. Whether or not you dig deeper into the work of Hall and Hofstede, I have found the tools in this chapter valuable in helping managers and professionals to understand each other better, clarify communication, and collaborate more effectively.

Having learned about the tools, the next step is to challenge yourself to apply the frameworks to multicultural scenarios. Use them to inspire more detailed inquiry into people whose backgrounds are different from yours and what assumptions and values may influence their perceptions and behaviors. At the same time, remember that these frameworks were developed from studies of entire cultures, so be alert to further variations by region, locality, socioeconomic class and so on. As you assemble teams and manage group interactions with this new understanding, I think you will find that balancing cultural differences, just like balancing gender, will help reduce conflicts and boost performance.

In my experience, bridging cultural differences is always more successful than trying to "change" them. That requires a give-and-take mindset where all sides make a genuine effort to "get" each other, respect pre-existing values and practices, and adapt in order to serve larger goals. When I had the opportunity to work in Saudi Arabia, I had to wear a veil, not use perfume, and have a body guard. That wasn't easy for me — but it probably wasn't easy for the Saudi men I worked with to adapt to aspects of my culture and gender either. Our business interactions were successful because we didn't let our differences become obstacles — we leveraged them to achieve more than we could have separately.

SECTION II
Reflections, Exercises, Tips and Takeaways

Reflections:

- What aspects of gender physiology, socialization, and culture were "new" to you in this section? (You might want to make a list to see how much you can remember.) How can you use this information to be a better manager and get more out of the teams and individuals you manage?

- Think about your team members and colleagues. Can you see any traits or behaviors that you've judged as "choices" that you now see have deeper roots in physiology, socialization or culture? What insights do you have about individual team members — and yourself — related to the impact of physiology, socialization and culture?

- Recall a recent meeting, project or team that worked well. Now look at the people involved in the context of what we've discussed. Did the situation work because of an appreciation and balance of members' different strengths — or because everyone on the team was similar? If the latter, what criteria can help you determine when similarity is beneficial and when diversity will produce better results?

- Recall a recent meeting, project or team that *didn't* work out well. Can you identify any conflicts, poor decisions, or performance issues that could be attributed to not addressing differences in physiology, socialization or culture?

- Think about a time when you or other team members dismissed a situation as "just a man-woman thing" or something similar related to differing cultures. Do the information and tools in Section II give you a better explanation? How could you more positively intervene in future situations?

Exercises:

- Based on what you learned in Chapter 3 and Chapter 4, create a short list of challenges you should anticipate and proactive steps you can take as a manager if your team is:
  — Women only or predominantly women
  — One or two women but predominantly male
  — Men only
- Identify the most effective ways to enhance *your* team's understanding and communication about gender and culture differences. Is it one-on-one coaching? Formal diversity training? Informal lunch-and-learns? A social event? Something else? Brainstorm some ideas, then draw up an actionable plan to implement one or propose it to senior management. Don't be afraid to draw on the expertise of your company's HR, organizational learning, or similar departments.
- Hofstede's cultural dimensions provide a good framework for a group activity. Prepare and distribute a brief explanation of them, then ask team members to place themselves on each dimensional spectrum. For example, if Small Power Distance is 1 and Large Power Distance is 10, I might say I'm a 4. You could also have team members rate each other before revealing how each person rated themselves. There are many ways to use this information to inspire good, open conversation about how we perceive (or mis-perceive) ourselves and each other.
- As a group exercise, review a recently completed project, event or period of time. Discuss:
  — How conflicts or misunderstandings were impacted by gender or culture differences
  — One thing related to gender or culture that made people uncomfortable
  — One thing related to gender or culture showing the positive side of having diverse perspectives represented
  — Suggestions for how to make future projects more inclusive and balanced while ensuring clear communications

- Perform a "gender/culture audit" for your department or work group:
    — What is the current breakdown by gender, age, cultural background?
    — What gender-related or culture-related "gaps" are creating challenges between team members?
    — What training or learning opportunities are currently available to team members when it comes to gender and culture differences?
    — How often do you as a manager reach out to people from different backgrounds to try to understand their perspective and make sure the work environment gives them the best opportunity to succeed?
    — What are the top improvement opportunities in terms of creating a more balanced, higher-performing team?
- Have your management team watch the *Frontline* program "The Warning" (http://video.pbs.org/video/1302794657/). Discuss how gender may have impacted the way Brooksley Born's warnings about the derivatives bubble were ignored. Discuss the value of gender-balanced leadership teams — and what you can do to achieve better balance.

Tips:

- *Do your pre-work.* The better you understand gender and culture differences *before* an engagement, the less chance there will be of a misunderstanding or irresolvable conflict. For example, I recently heard about an American business team that went to an important meeting in a Scandinavian country and interpreted their counterparts' nodding as assent. However, in this country and others, nodding simply signifies "yes, we are listening." The Americans returned home claiming they had negotiated numerous verbal agreements — which the Scandinavians promptly refuted. A little preparation would have avoided this misinterpretation and its repercussions!

- *Take nothing for granted.* Oversimplifying gender and culture can lead to mistakes. For example, my native language is Spanish. If you looked at my background and skills, even before I began international consulting, you might assume I'd be a perfect fit for assignments in Latin America or Spain. You would be right in some ways — but wrong in others. You see, I learned Caribbean Spanish — a mix of Spanish, native Caribbean Indian and African dialects. Similarly, my cultural background, as discussed in this book's Introduction, is more complex than my bloodline. So yes, I can navigate Latin America with greater ease than someone with a pure Anglo background. But it is still important to do my homework and approach distinct Latin American markets with an open mind. I can tell you from personal experience that "my" Spanish and cultural signifiers are not identical to what is found in Venezuela, Colombia, Argentina, Chile and so on.
- *Be diligent and inquisitive.* Never forget that our behavioral DNA is almost as complex as our actual DNA — and includes not just national culture, but regional culture, local culture, culture related to groups, personal variations and more. This book gives you good tools to help analyze that DNA and make decisions accordingly, but an ongoing desire to understand is the greatest tool of all.
- *Leverage a range of resources.* Culture and its impact in the workplace are complex, so it is wise to sample an array of resources to broaden your perspective and create a more complete and accurate framework for understanding. One excellent resource you shouldn't overlook: other people. Reach out to those from other cultures in your organization and schedule some social time where you can learn about each other's backgrounds. If you have family or friends who travel extensively or have more experience than you managing a multicultural workforce, invite them to share their insights. There is a good chance that your organization has existing resources to improve multicultural understanding, often through the HR department, and you can also

recommend that the company send you to seminars or training as part of your professional development. Last but not least, there are many excellent books, articles and studies on culture, including those cited in this section. If something raises your curiosity, check the source in the References section and read it yourself. Usually, these sources will in turn link you to additional resources. Before you know it, you'll be one of your organization's "culture experts"!

Takeaways:

1. Your performance as a manager can benefit significantly from the scientific research now available on gender and cultural differences and how they impact individual behavior and workplace dynamics. The convergence of related fields of study into emerging disciplines such as socio-economics is generating particularly valuable insights for business leaders.

2. Differing socialization processes for girls and boys still define roles, expectations and stereotypes that impact the way men and women relate at work. By becoming aware of gender-based behavioral tendencies and learning how to manage them you can help create a gender-smart work environment that reduces conflicts and misunderstandings and leverages the complementary strengths of men and women.

3. In today's increasingly multicultural workforce, the impact of cultural differences on how individuals respond and interact at work cannot be ignored. Creating an inclusive, respectful environment is essential — and it is equally important to make sure you and your team understand the different values and assumptions that drive people from different cultures.

SECTION III — CONSEQUENCES

Underperforming Individuals and Companies: The Price of Ignoring Gender and Culture Differences

From my firm's consulting work, I know that the topics covered in the first two sections of this book create discomfort for many men and women. There is a natural "pushback" when we present material at odds with a person's prior assumptions and experiences. The challenge is exacerbated by the legal, social and workplace structures that condition us to "avoid" talking about our differences in a direct and honest way.

If you've been struggling in these respects, it may help to remember a shared intention and goal of senior executives, managers, legislators, high-performing individuals of any gender or culture, and leadership consultants like me: to maximize individual and organizational performance.

Isn't that the "spirit" behind legislative and corporate efforts to achieve "equal opportunity"? Isn't that why large amounts of money are spent to recruit and develop talented women and minorities? Isn't that why companies bring in consultants to help them understand the cultures where they want to do business? Isn't that why you're reading this book?

In my work, I start from the premise that almost everyone shares the goal of improving individual and organizational performance. If approaches used in the past were driving such improvements, we could all rest easy. But too often past approaches, though well-intended, have not delivered the results we want. We must therefore challenge those approaches, and ourselves — not to affix blame or make anyone uncomfortable, but to break free of what's kept us "stuck" and find a new path forward.

In the first two sections of this book, we looked at the historical forces and trends shaping today's diverse workforce, as well as the physiological, social and cultural differences that impact behaviors and interactions.

Keeping this foundational knowledge in mind, let's now explore how gender and cultural differences manifest as workforce challenges.

As a manager, you probably have firsthand experience of many of the challenges I'll present in this section. Perhaps you have found them frustrating and difficult to comprehend in the past. But with a more accurate and complete understanding of our differences, we can now confront the challenges head on and develop solutions rooted in reality rather than misperceptions and flawed "treat everyone the same" tactics.

Chapter 6 will explore nine gender-related challenges I have witnessed everywhere my work has taken me. By "gender-related challenges," I do not mean "women need to be fixed" to reach their potential and advance into top leadership positions. On the contrary, these challenges are external and systemic as much as internal — and they create confusion, unhappiness, miscommunication and underperformance for everyone, not just women. Combining my own experience and advice with relevant research in diverse fields such as sociology, economics, anthropology, and organizational behavior, my goal is to help men and women open up a more productive dialogue that can help us get beyond these challenges.

In Chapter 7, I will address four top-level obstacles that prevent companies and managers from getting the most out of a multicultural workforce. Here again, the focus is not "how can we get them to be more like us" — the hard truth is that we must shift our personal mindsets and organizational paradigms in order to succeed.

My research for *Can You Afford to Ignore Me?* confirmed what I knew from years of consulting experience and work with leadership issues: Ignoring gender and cultural differences and trying to create genderless, culture-less environments is not a sustainable model. In fact, this approach contributes to a host of problems that many companies face: poor morale, disappointing productivity, failure to attract and retain top talent, legal liability, and more.

Now the good news. A convincing body of research also shows that balanced, diverse work environments and leadership teams consistently lead to better performance. To cite one recent example, an article in the April 2012 *McKinsey Quarterly* reported impressive results from a study of 180 publicly traded companies in Europe and the U.S. Among other findings, companies in the top quartile for executive board diversity (women and foreign nationals) had a 53% higher return on equity than those in the bottom quartile.[47] In short, beyond legal and ethical concerns, companies should pay attention to diversity as a bottom-line strategic issue and competitive differentiator.

What about global companies that *have* invested in coaching, training, and diversity initiatives, but haven't achieved the improvements they want? In many cases, the problem is that they are spending money on programs for discrete groups of employees, but not addressing the root causes and systemic structures that keep producing the same unwanted work dynamics and challenges. I qualify my work with clients by emphasizing that helping individuals understand the origins of gender and culture differences, or doing a seminar to dispel stereotypes, or working to clarify career paths for women and those from other cultures — this is all important, but it's just the beginning of the journey. Real, lasting change happens when everyone — from the top tier down — works proactively toward a gender-smart, culturally sensitive workplace.

When companies embrace this as a strategic business objective, a new mindset begins to permeate the corporate culture. As the leadership of a company adjusts its approach, so too individual managers and professionals become willing to adjust their mindsets and reframe expectations in a way that is good for everyone.

So, if you have been struggling, please "park" your doubting inner voice a little longer. This section will help you tie some things together and bring what we've discussed closer to your work experiences. Remember that our shared goal is to improve performance — yours, your team's, your colleagues', your company's. Understanding and overcoming gender and cultural challenges will help you make real progress toward that goal.

Can you afford not to?

CHAPTER 6
Nine Gender-Related Challenges
No Company Can Afford to Ignore

My curiosity and my professional work have long revolved around certain questions: What keeps companies from promoting more women? What is missing in leadership programs for women? Why are work relationships between men and women still difficult and fraught with misunderstanding? What are the real reasons that so many talented women derail from promising career paths or "give up" on their corporations?

My initial assumption was that such questions would have different answers in different cultures. Experience taught me otherwise. Having worked in many parts of the world, I have found that the nine challenges in this chapter are universal.

Culture *is* a factor in how we manage and develop talent. Norms in some cultures certainly exacerbate challenges for women, while others ease the impact by promoting dialogue and embracing gender-balanced environments. So the challenges vary in intensity in different cultures and workplaces — but they are almost always present in the social, cultural, and structural paradigm that women experience at work.

There is a tendency to approach these issues separately, and detached from any larger gender context. The company provides Maria with training in a specific area, or assigns her a mentor, and that's the end of the story. However, this approach rarely increases the number of women in leadership positions. To achieve *that* goal, we need to look at the big picture. The nine challenges I've identified are commingled — they impact different women at different stages of their lives and careers, and they are inextricably linked to the gender differences we've been discussing throughout this book.

Everyone in today's workforce needs to become more aware of these challenges. In my corporate consulting engagements, I find that just getting the challenges out in the open and raising the right questions leads to practical insights for all involved. Often it sparks a realization that prior efforts at training or mentoring weren't effective because other systemic or personal challenges weren't addressed.

In my coaching work with individual women, I have developed a number of ways to work through these challenges, and I will share relevant tips throughout the chapter. A committed manager can be transformative coaching a woman to reframe her potential, calibrate her perceptions and behaviors, and map out a path to a leadership position. But organizations and managers must also understand that they need to proactively work toward a gender-smart workplace where such transformations are encouraged and rewarded. Balance is critical, and men must be as much a part of the dialogue as women.

After all, gender-related challenges don't just hold back female employees, they impair the performance of teams, departments and the business. Similarly, when you untangle these issues, the victory isn't just Maria realizing her potential — it's you and your team gaining an understanding and ease with one another that will help resolve conflict, clarify communication, increase engagement and commitment, and tap synergies that can improve almost any area of business. Plus, many of the skills and insights you develop on the path to becoming "gender smart" will help you understand and manage cultural issues more effectively as well.

Why waste any more time going around and around on the same issues without making progress? Let's look at them directly, understand them fully, and begin moving toward a more engaged, better aligned workplace.

Double Bind: Held Back by Contradictory Demands

I said in this chapter's introduction that we need to keep all nine challenges in front of us, but in some ways, the first challenge runs through all the others. To help women succeed, we must understand that social and cultural forces often put them in no-win situations — a "double bind" — as they try to advance their careers. Many experts have referenced this double bind, including Pat Heim, and Catalyst offers an excellent report titled "The Double-Bind Dilemma for Women in Leadership." But let's start with *The American Heritage Dictionary* definition of double bind:

1. A psychological impasse created when contradictory demands are made of an individual, so that no matter which directive is followed, the response will be construed as incorrect. **2.** A situation in which a person must choose between equally unsatisfactory alternatives; a punishing and inescapable dilemma.[48]

Recall what we learned about socialization in Chapter 4. Society gives each gender a set of expectations and rules that define how to behave, interact and participate in the world. Girls are told to be nice, share power, be supportive and prevent conflict. Boys are expected to be assertive, competitive, and take the lead.

In some contexts, that socialization process may be seen as attuning men and women to natural tendencies that come from physiological differences. But most workplaces still operate according to male principles and values — which creates numerous "double bind" problems for women:

- If a woman emulates assertive male behaviors, both men and women become suspicious and feel she is too pushy
- If a woman is collaborative and inclusive, sharing power and seeking consensus, she is perceived as weak and unable to make decisions
- If a woman shows passion, men dismiss her as too emotional

Leaders at most companies say they want to build an inclusive culture, promote equal opportunity and access to power, and advance women through their leadership pipeline, but this intention will never become reality if the double binds of the underlying social context aren't addressed.

In my work in the U.S. and in international markets, I find the double bind for women at the core of many miscommunications and conflicts. In individual interactions as well as the corporate culture as a whole, it creates problems for everyone, undermines overall performance and leads to functional paralysis in many situations. To overcome this challenge, both sides need to accept that men and women see the world through different filters — but also focus on the shared goal of having better, more productive work relationships that lead to personal and organizational success.

To get moving in the right direction, women must become aware — and must hear from their managers — that their true strength is in authentic behavior, not in trying to copy male behaviors that are unnatural to them. From the other side, men should challenge the stereotypes and preconceived notions that make most work environments so rigidly "male" and instead seek a more balanced, collaborative dialogue. When male managers and team members self-regulate certain behaviors and drop old assumptions about how women should or should not behave, interactions with female peers and direct reports will invariably become easier and more effective.

Another critical aspect of "unbinding" the double bind involves relationships between women, and in particular how women respond to other women in leadership positions. Female team members must learn to self-regulate their typically negative reactions to women managers who are direct or assertive, so that they can support the advancement of female colleagues rather than sabotage it.

To offer a simple example that I have seen again and again: If a male manager approaches a female assistant and tells her "I need this memo by 3 p.m.," the odds are high that the work will get done, no questions asked. But if a female manager makes the same statement in the same tone, the female assistant will be taken aback: "Who does she think she is 'commanding' me to do something?"

I'll continue exploring the issue of women undermining each other in the next section, but for now, the key point is that a "double bind" for women in the workforce is the natural by-product of both male and female socialization. As a manager, you have to be alert to this and challenge all team members to question their cultural programming and consider new ways of perceiving female leadership.

We can't afford the counterproductive effects of the double bind for women. Today's business reality demands that men and women combine their complementary personal qualities and skills. That starts with a candid, open approach to the behaviors and experiences that make us different. Different is good! When embraced, our differences become strengths rather than challenges. Appreciating and leveraging these differences yields better work performance, and also strengthens our long-term relationships and professional networks.

The Dragon Lady: What Shapes Her and Why She Is Rejected

One consequence of the double bind I just discussed is that some women not only emulate male behavior, they overcompensate and become what are sometimes referred to as "dragon ladies."

The term "dragon lady" has a range of meanings in different contexts, but most are a variation on what we find in *Merriam-Webster*: "an over-bearing or tyrannical woman."[49]

This is certainly not a politically correct term — some understandably find it offensive! But I risk using it because I want to make sure I have people's attention, even if I provoke discomfort or "pushback." The issues around this persona are too important and pervasive to ignore, and they won't be resolved by walking on eggshells.

The "dragon lady" manifests in both male-female and female-female relationships, and I have found her in literally every region I have worked in. When I introduce the concept, I inevitably get an immediate reaction from the audience, irrespective of cultural origin.

Why does a woman who wants to be successful in business feel she must become a dragon lady? And why are so many women categorized this way — sometimes unfairly? Once again we have to return to the challenging reality of women being socialized and physiologically predisposed toward flattened relationships, empathy, playing nice and so on — but then entering corporate environments where those traits are perceived (and experienced!) as potential liabilities. Trying to achieve status in such environments, some women understandably emulate what many categorize as "male behavior." After this approach helps them achieve some status, they up the ante in hopes of attaining more.

In essence, the dragon lady becomes a social hybrid — grafting more and more "male- like behavior" onto herself as she tries to climb the corporate ladder. The strategy works up to a point, but then it hits a wall. The problem — which is both behavioral on the dragon lady's part and perceptual in the culture's — is that this behavior strikes men and women as *too* assertive, domineering, arrogant, and impersonal.

Far from welcoming this male-adapted woman into their ranks, appreciating the time and talent she has committed, and rewarding her willingness to sacrifice her authentic self in order to be "one of the guys," most men keep their distance from a dragon lady and feel she can only be trusted up to a certain level of power.

Women tend to outright reject a dragon lady — in part because they feel she has rejected them. Excluded from the inner circles of men and women, peers and subordinates alike, dragon ladies don't get the support, loyalty and networking strength they need to reach the next level. Fending for themselves, they get stuck on a plateau with an unanswerable question: What else must I do to get a corner office?

As an example from my experience, I was once hired to do training by a female vice president at a multinational company. She was highly intelligent, very assertive, and some would say boastful. During a break from one training session, she complained to me that she was not getting the promotion she deserved. The company's CEO happened to join us as she was noting her abilities and professional attributes, and his response was quite illuminating. He said that as women move up in a corporation, they need to understand that masculine behaviors and attributes that they felt were necessary to make their initial footprints are no longer needed among their new peers and may be detrimental in their new roles. It was not hard to read between the lines. I believe that one reason this woman was not getting her promotion was that she had transformed herself into such a dragon lady that the CEO felt people had a hard time working with her and wouldn't respond to her as a top-level leader.

However, another aspect of the dragon lady phenomenon involves female workplace relationships in general. Recall how women are socialized. While boys are taught that it's good to compete and stand out, the key to early interactions for girls is to treat all as equals and "play nice." That expectation carries forward into adulthood. When a woman breaks the paradigm, in attitude or by earning singular promotions, her former peers often feel left out and become resentful of her power and recognition.

Author, consultant and teacher Dr. Pat Heim calls this the "power dead-even rule."[50] The backlash from breaking the rule creates a damaging social disequilibrium among women. If a woman gets promoted, and fails to proactively reaffirm relationships and signal connection to female peers, she may find herself excluded directly or indirectly from social interactions she once had and cherished as part of her work experience. Sometimes she must even resort to outright "apologizing," as if her success is somehow an affront to other women. Even if the promotion did not come from emulating male behaviors, they may perceive that she is now "different" and unreachable. Deserved or not, breaking the dead-even rule can make a woman a "dragon lady" in the eyes of female co-workers.

Numerous books, articles and studies have explored this and related topics, but let me summarize a few of the most salient points that managers should keep in mind:

- When a woman is promoted, other women tend to withdraw support from her. This unfortunately reinforces a perception among some male managers that there is no way to please female employees. It's bad if women do not get promoted, but there are also problems if they do.
- Facebook COO Sheryl Sandberg cut to the heart of the issue at the Davos 2012 World Economic Forum, explaining that "success and likability are positively correlated for men and negatively correlated for women. The more power a man gets, the more he is liked. The more power a woman gets, the less she is liked."[51]
- Women tend to be more rigid and demanding when dealing with other women. They evaluate other women's work and behavior more rigorously than they evaluate men, and are less tolerant of failure and mistakes among women.
- Many women shy away from asking for stretch assignments that showcase their talents and expertise because it might make them look "too ambitious" and isolate them from a sense of comfort and social networks at work and in their personal lives.

Clearly, in terms of performance and the strength of a corporate culture, dealing with the occasional dragon lady is just the tip of the iceberg. It is just as damaging when women limit themselves in order *not* to be seen as dragon ladies! In fact, the closer we look at the "dragon lady" challenge, the more we see it is the symptom of a deeper problem: work environments where a large percentage of people, male and female, do not feel they can "just be themselves."

To achieve higher performance, we need to make it possible for individuals to be authentic and leverage their personal strengths. We need to create gender-smart work environments where different masculine and feminine qualities are encouraged, developed — and compensated with full parity.

We all have to unlearn the assumptions and behaviors that prevent us from achieving that balance and taking advantage of the opportunities that surround us. One key is for senior executives and managers to make sure that the corporate culture and promotion practices don't send the message that the only way to succeed is to "be pushy and demanding." In other words, instead of telling women that they must become male-adapted "dragon ladies" to succeed, we need to put out the message that leadership attributes that tend to be specific to females are just as valued as commonly male attributes.

One book I recommend in that regard is *Through the Labyrinth: The Truth About How Women Become Leaders* by Alice H. Eagly and Linda L. Carli. The authors make a powerful case that female attributes like collaboration, tolerance and inclusivity are extremely valuable for 21st century businesses and should be driving hiring decisions, succession plans and more.[52]

Breaking free of the "dragon lady" challenge is not just about ambitious women giving up their male-adapted behaviors, it is also about *all* women looking at how they treat other women. In particular, women need to disentangle themselves from the "dead-even rule" and recalibrate their behavior to celebrate, not sabotage, the success of female colleagues. Lois P. Frankel makes an excellent related point in her book *Nice Girls Don't Get the Corner Office*: "Success comes not from acting more like a man…but by acting more like a *woman* instead of a girl."[53] In other words, by dropping "girlish" behaviors rooted in childhood socialization and seeking a more mature, affirming gender dialogue, women can embrace their unique strengths, promote the power of personal branding and self-development, and reassure each other that the price of success will not be social reprisal and isolation.

One of the pillars holding up the "glass ceiling" is that when women get promoted, they lose support precisely when it is needed to rise further. Given these conditions, is it any surprise that so many stall as mid-level "dragon ladies" and never get a corner office?

Feeling (and *Being*) Unheard

When my firm starts a training or consulting engagement with women, we like to ask two questions:

- When you share an idea or suggestion with your team or peers, particularly the men, do they give you attention and credit for your contributions?
- If the same idea is articulated by a man or your boss, does it receive a better response — does the team, especially the men, listen in a way they didn't listen to you?

What we consistently hear is a chorus of "I'm not heard!" Women tell us they have to repeat themselves to get attention, that their ideas are not embraced as quickly or emphatically as similar ideas presented by men — and that they are very frustrated.

Why do women feel unheard? Do men purposely tune them out? Let's see if we can identify the barriers — so we can begin to remove them.

Some believe the language itself could be one such barrier. As early as 1905, Otto Jespersen described the English language as "positively and expressly masculine, it is the language of a grown-up man and has very little childish or feminine about it."[54] Many linguists and theorists from widely divergent perspectives have classified English as a masculine language since then. Without getting too deeply into the details of that linguistic debate, it does seem important to consider the possibility that women are unheard and workplace communications between genders go awry at least in part because the communication model is marinated in testosterone!

Regardless of the role the language itself may play, numerous studies have confirmed a communication gender bias. A man's speech, written work, meeting contributions, etc. tend to be perceived as more important, trustworthy, competent and persuasive. Some theorists have suggested that feminine language and speaking styles are not well-suited to business environments. Others have shown that masculine/feminine aspects of language tend to correlate with dominant/subordinate positions.

But for now let's hone in on a more practical comparison of typical male and female communication modes. In my consulting work, I have found that this is where we are most able to raise awareness and then make adjustments — both as speakers and listeners — that move us closer to a state of communication equity.

We have discussed the impact of socialization — and in communication, it is again true that differences in how boys and girls are raised lead to expectations, perceptions and behaviors that continue to polarize us as adults. For example, from an early age, boys are praised for calling out answers in school and asserting themselves in social situations while girls are urged to "wait their turn" to talk or share ideas. In the workplace, the former mode is more valued and better rewarded — an ability to "interrupt" and assert one's views is essential. Most men acquire that ability early in life, but many women have the double disadvantage of being tolerant of others' interruptions *and* uncomfortable being an interrupter. The logical result is that they make fewer contributions than male counterparts who have no problem interrupting or shutting down outside suggestions. The dynamic here has an additional negative — sometimes women's failure to interrupt is mistranslated as approval.

Digging deeper into the impact of socialization, women traditionally view communication as a process to exchange favors and support. They tend to use indirect language, with a vocabulary that seeks consensus — "we" is preferred to "I." They ask more questions, play down personal accomplishments, and use language to democratize an environment. Even if a woman carried the weight in a project's success, she is likely to say "we all did it together."

Men on the other hand often see communication as a tool for showcasing their power, exercising control, or gaining the upper hand in a situation. They use direct language, are more concise, and comfortably slide into command mode. They state or tell more than they question, and are quick to tout their personal impact and accomplishments. In some cases, they may even take credit, explicitly or implicitly, for the ideas of others. Such situations point up the importance of women being able to compete for power and claim what is rightfully theirs. I teach the women I coach that if one of their ideas is put forward by someone else, they should make a point of clarifying this to the audience by saying something like "Jim, thank you for sharing my suggestion" and then move on.

Voice and tone also have an impact. Most women have high-pitched voices, which are indirectly associated with children. Women's voices also have greater dynamism — they use more pitch tones (five) when talking, and the variation tends to be "heard" as emotional rather than authoritative. In addition, for both physical and social reasons, women tend to speak more softly — again implying docile or passive behavior.

Men use only three tones in their voice pitch, giving the impression of control, centeredness, and power. Underscoring the potential impact of this difference, a study published in the *Proceedings of The Royal Society B: Biological Sciences* found that voters choosing between hypothetical political candidates consistently chose the one with the deeper voice. As the study concludes, "men and women with lower-pitched voices may be more successful in obtaining positions of leadership. This might also suggest that because women, on average, have higher-pitched voices than men, voice pitch could be a factor that contributes to fewer women holding leadership roles."[55]

As has been well-documented, Margaret Thatcher understood this so clearly that she invested an enormous amount of time and energy on elocution lessons — radically modifying everything from vocal pitch and tone to modulation and pacing, and suppressing her regional accent — in order to facilitate larger groups of people finding her credible and appealing as a leader.

I'm not implying that a woman must be as driven as "the Iron Lady" to get the credit and organizational advancement she deserves. The point is that there *are* specific ways to improve our ability to be heard — but we have to first understand and be attentive to our audience to know what adjustments will be most effective. These are teachable skills, and managers often tell me they are pleasantly surprised by how much an employee's performance improves after a little coaching on "being heard." Obviously, it is very empowering for individual women as well!

Expertise Is Second-Guessed or Ignored

In the "Exercises" at the end of Section II, I recommended having your management team watch and discuss the *Frontline* program "The Warning." In the context of this book, a key revelation in the program is that Brooksley Born, the female Chairperson of the Commodities Future Trading Commission (CFTC) from 1996 to 1999, gave ample warnings about the unregulated over-the-counter derivatives market that eventually led to the 2008 financial crisis — but she was ignored.

The story has *many* lessons about why female leaders get second-guessed and shut out of critical decisions. First, it typically has nothing to do with their level of expertise. In Born's case, before accepting the CFTC position she had been a lawyer for 20 years *specializing* in derivatives and enjoyed an excellent international reputation. It is also clear that she had done her homework and accumulated solid evidence for her arguments.

So, are women like Born ignored just *because* they are women? That would be an oversimplification. Yes, flat-out gender bias frequently plays a role. Born was a lone female among a group of male economic leaders. In the video, then-Chairman of the SEC Arthur Levitt admits that, while he didn't know Born at the time, the other men told him she was "irascible, difficult, stubborn, unreasonable."[56] That's a classic case of men dismissing a woman in power as a "dragon lady" who can't be trusted.

But women's expertise gets ignored for many other reasons as well — and the "corrective actions" involve the assumptions and behaviors of individual women as well as cultural biases against female leadership.

For example, the Born story is a profound illustration of the dangers of "group think." Whether a "group" is defined by gender, culture, social class, ideology or other factors, resisting "outside" perspectives results in poor decisions that negatively impact project outcomes, corporate performance, and even, in Born's case, the entire global economy! So, certainly, managers should create environments where diverse perspectives and expertise are invited and respected. However, I also tell the women I coach that, so far as they *are* the outside perspective, they must understand the system of power they're part of and take appropriate action to ensure that their expertise is received *as* expertise.

Without conjecturing about Born specifically, many women in similar positions make the mistake of believing that intellectual capital and a detailed presentation of the facts are enough to earn their views full consideration. This is rarely the case. Strategic networking, which I'll devote a whole section to later in this chapter, is a "must." When many people know a woman at a personal level and are confident in her competence, her ideas will have more credibility and traction. Conversely, if few people truly "know" her, the chances of being heard drop significantly.

Similarly, even the most carefully researched details may get second-guessed if the presentation *style* is ineffective. I remind women that in order to win respect for our expertise we must know how and when to *assert* it.

As a manager, you must be aware of all sides of this complex challenge — including the fact that females are often more prone to second-guessing each other, and themselves, than males are. Coaching individual women on how to trust and deliver their expertise may be as important as intervening during a meeting to make sure a female viewpoint is not dismissed. But a great first step is to set the right example yourself: Treat expertise as expertise, regardless of gender, and insist that the rest of your team adopt the same mindset.

"She's Not Good at Delegating"

Leadership skills are defined in various ways, and obviously depend on organizational context, but one quality is a constant: the ability to delegate. Those adept at delegating — assigning tasks, teaching others and giving them the space to learn from their own mistakes — are understandably looked at as good management material.

Many women struggle with delegating for a number of reasons. One of their natural assets — the ability to multitask — can be a liability in this area. As multitasking has become highly desirable in today's workforce, women may feel they can best prove their worth by being overachievers and keeping all the work to themselves. They may do well in this regard and earn the appreciation of superiors and peers — but their apparent unwillingness to delegate work to others becomes a huge impediment if they aspire to move up the corporate ladder.

Social mandates are also a factor. The desire to avoid conflict and "not be bossy" may prevent a woman from farming out work because she doesn't want to be perceived as telling others what to do and giving orders. Even when women do delegate, they may find it uncomfortable and politically difficult in ways that impact their ability to do it *effectively*.

In a *Times Higher Education* article on a study she did about senior management skills, Professor Barbara Bagilhole identifies another factor: "While there is a stereotypical perception that women don't like to delegate because of a need for control, they may find delegation hard because they are in an all-male environment that is not supportive."[57]

In my experience, all these factors come into play, and there is one more that merits special attention. Women often feel a need to demonstrate their abilities beyond any doubt — to achieve "perfection." Delegation, in this context, presents the risk that someone else's performance may cause the project to fall short of perfection.

Pat Heim's *In the Company of Women* provides further insight on this topic. She notes that "study after study find that women outscore men in most management categories," but risk-taking and delegating are two traditional areas of weakness. Why? "When we were girls, many of our teachers encouraged us to focus on details and praised us for neatness, good penmanship and following the rules. In our minds, perfection became an attainable ideal. Most likely, at the same time we were also discouraged from taking risks for fear of producing imperfect work." As she points out, this perfectionist mindset prompts a tendency to micromanage rather than delegate.[58]

Managerial guidance can be invaluable in helping women confront this challenge — first and foremost by opening up a frank dialogue to help them understand that perfectionism and an inability to delegate negatively impact their opportunities to move into higher managerial roles. Returning to Professor Bagilhole's point, you should also look at how supportive or unsupportive your work environment is for women. You may need to help a female manager understand and navigate the company's internal politics, or develop a strategy to reassure her that delegating will not get her into trouble. It is also imperative to help women recalibrate their standards away from the kind of perfectionism that ultimately creates paralysis and self-doubt.

One simple, practical way that I help women I'm coaching in this area is to lead them through a side-by-side comparison. I ask them to give me an example of a situation where a male colleague made a noticeable mistake — a typo in a PowerPoint presentation, misquoting a figure, etc. Then I ask how the mistake was handled. Almost inevitably, the woman says that the man just moved on, barely acknowledging anything, and made a "correction" if necessary during a post-presentation Q&A or via a later email or phone call. The lesson I drive home is that the real goal is a successful overall outcome. That requires diligence, competency and hard work — but trying to perfect every detail will not matter if you fail to close the deal or finish the project.

I also emphasize that hoarding tasks in the pursuit of individual perfection has negative consequences from an organizational perspective. Most importantly, when you don't delegate, you miss a vital strategic tool that ensures knowledge transfer. Passing tasks on to others, and giving them the necessary information and coaching rather than just "doing it yourself," is the best way to create the organizational depth that will ensure smooth transitions when someone is promoted or takes on a new project or initiative. In that sense, failure to delegate can even create one more obstacle to a woman being promoted — if she's made it seem like she's the only person who can do her present job, how can the company afford to move her to another position?

Perfection is impossible to attain — and therefore very stressful to carry as your benchmark! Female professionals will experience a great sense of relief if you can help them shift their focus from "perfection" to striving for excellent outcomes that take into account imperfect realities. Liberated from the "self-talk" that fears every little mistake and tells them they must control every detail, they will find it much easier to delegate. Simultaneously, they will begin to evolve from a purely tactical approach to a more strategic mindset. In short, they will have more of what it takes to advance through your leadership pipeline.

Understanding the Importance of Strategic Networking

I once worked with a woman employed by a large pharmaceutical firm. She had been raised to think that it was improper to invite herself to any event. Projecting this social context onto her work context, she didn't invite herself to meetings or to higher levels of corporate participation — and felt bad that she rarely *got* invited. I suggested that invitation in the corporate arena is often a two-way street and helped her separate what was "proper" at work from how she had been raised. We examined the consequences to her team and company of not having her data, experience and knowledge in meetings and decision-making processes where they clearly belonged. I also helped her depersonalize the invitation issue by pointing out that in a large global company like hers, everyone tends to be extremely busy and specialized, so they are not always aware of what others do or could bring to the table. In essence, it is one's responsibility to flag others when you can contribute valuable knowledge.

Sure enough, once she began inviting herself into conversations and meetings, she also got more invitations in return. As a result, she was able to make better connections throughout the organization, which benefited not only her career but also the company.

This example illustrates another common challenge: Most women have difficulty developing and understanding the need for strategic networking.

For women like the one in my story, this is often because they are constrained by a social norm that says it is rude to invite yourself to a meeting or event. In other cases, it is a matter of doubting one's worth. Some women think, "if they wanted me to be involved, they would have invited me" or "senior executives are too busy to set aside time to talk with someone like me."

Many confident, assertive women fail to engage in strategic networking for another reason: They don't believe it is important. Raised to embrace flattened, democratic relationships where success is shared, women assume that if they work hard and demonstrate their talent, word will spread naturally and they will receive the recognition and promotions they deserve. With many women juggling work and family responsibilities, networking may seem a waste of precious time — a social activity that has little professional impact or payoff.

What most successful people understand, and what research has consistently shown, is that the reality is just the opposite. Strategic networking — extending your connections and presence outside the scope of your daily tasks — is absolutely critical to career advancement. One study of HR specialists made this point explicitly — when two candidates had similar backgrounds and experience, the one with more contacts and better social connections usually got the job or promotion.

In a *Times Higher Education* article on strategic networking, Dr. Barbara Bagilhole draws the same basic conclusion from a study of the field of higher education: "Success is not achieved by publishing more or even doing better research, but through personal contacts, friendship, and cooperative work with key players in the field. Women like to work collaboratively and cooperatively, but we have to think about this strategically. Women need to promote each other and themselves."[59]

The same can be said in almost any professional field. Working hard and demonstrating your skills and intellectual capacity will only get you so far. At a certain plateau, these qualities are trumped by social and networking skills — and women who haven't embraced that part of career-building suddenly find themselves stuck.

I have witnessed *many* women in exactly that situation. Female lawyers wait, expecting that if they consistently write perfect briefs and win court cases, they will make partner. Female engineers wait, assuming that hard work, dedication, and good project outcomes will drive the next promotion. When the "wait" proves endless, many exit the organization angry and confused. They mistakenly thought they were doing all the right things — and overlooked the one activity necessary to reach the next level. They had a blind spot regarding the influence of networking on their upward mobility.

The impact of that blind spot is confirmed by feedback I often get from senior managers before I start a coaching engagement. The first concern they state during these sessions consistently involves a lack of networking connections or political capital, and a failure to understand how important this is for promotions, stretch assignments and career-building. The women haven't grasped that to reach the next tier in the corporate structure, they must commit themselves to developing personal connections with as many well-positioned stakeholders as possible.

Women and their managers need to pay attention to three important functions of strategic networking, and get past any misunderstandings or obstacles preventing an individual from tapping into these functions. First, and most obviously, networking creates pathways for a talented professional to get to know people throughout the organization — and *be* known. When I coach women we talk about building a personal brand — and using networking to get the brand out there. Whether direct reports, upper management, key customers or partners, the goal is to have a "name" and a presence. You are no longer just another employee, you are Mary, who is known for certain unique strengths and qualities.

The second function of networking is equally important: to hear feedback from others, and gain a better perspective of your value to the organization. This is especially important for women, who tend to thrive on outside recognition, particularly from people who are role models or in positions of power. This is an area where managers should be proactive. Don't wait for Mary to reach out to you — if you noticed that she did a great job on a project, or have heard good things about her from others, take the time to network with her and tell her. Knowing that others think highly of her will boost self-confidence, deepen engagement, improve productivity, and encourage her to challenge herself to reach new heights.

The third important function involves knowledge transfer. In many organizations, workers who have been in the forefront of developing key products or services are hitting retirement age. Others may be reassigned or relocated for long periods of time. It is critical to have new workers connect with these people and absorb their knowledge so they can step in when someone moves on. Strategic networking is one of the best ways that a promising female professional can learn about the roles and work of people throughout the organization, tap into valuable knowledge, and be prepared to move into other positions when the opportunity arises.

As a manager, there are many simple ways to promote strategic networking — for those on your team, and cross-functionally as well. With regard to women specifically, a good starting point is to reach out to talented females and make sure they understand the value and even "necessity" of strategic networking. Emphasize to Mary that people need to know her in order to better understand her abilities and potential, and to give her deserved recognition and constructive feedback on areas for improvement. Unless she has a critical mass of people throughout the organization who know her, the possibilities for self-promoting and career advancement will be compromised.

On a practical level, women may also need guidance in *how* to network. One approach I use is to ask the woman I'm coaching to make a list of *all* the people who in any way can impact her present or future professional development. Once the list is done, we then develop a strategy on when and how to approach each person. This simplifies and demystifies the process, reducing the nebulous and perhaps intimidating concept of "networking" to a series of very do-able tasks. Having a tangible, self-created list of people who will influence her career path also gives the woman more of a sense of direction and inner control.

114

It is a real joy when I get emails and phone calls from the women I coach telling me how surprised they were that a top executive accepted a networking invitation, or how much they've learned by networking. Once they get through the first couple "cold calls" in their strategic networking assignments, they begin to see the value and embrace the activity as a rewarding part of their professional development.

Mentoring Challenges for Women

Mentoring is a key factor in the degree of success for most professionals, impacting the velocity of career development, organizational knowledge transfer, the accumulation of internal political capital, positioning for key assignments and promotions, and more. Unfortunately, for many of the same reasons that women struggle with networking, they also find it difficult to secure and fully leverage mentoring relationships.

I hear about "mentoring gaps" from both senior executives and the women I coach, so it is not surprising that a Catalyst report on women in leadership found that it was one of the top five barriers to women's advancement. In a survey of 500 senior women in large corporations and professional firms across Europe, 61% of respondents agreed or strongly agreed that "lack of mentoring" was a barrier. 64% identified a closely related barrier: "lack of senior or visibly successful female role models." In case you're curious, the survey's number one barrier (66%) was "stereotypes and preconceptions of women's roles and abilities."[60]

For talented women, the benefits of a strong mentoring relationship can be enormous. In a pertinent article in the *Financial Times*, Sylvia Hewlett makes the case that mentoring or sponsorship is often the "final push that can break the glass ceiling." The article is careful to distinguish between the kinds of relationships that involve "friendly advice" and the active advocacy of someone in a higher position of power. According to the data reported by Hewlett, "a powerful executive sponsor...prepared to go out on a limb for a chosen protégé and push for their next promotion" boosts the prospect of advancement by 23% for men and 19% for women.[61]

I should note that some now separate "mentors" from "sponsors" or "stewards," with the latter titles implying a commitment to not only offer guidance, but also actively champion on a person's behalf, including exposure to strategic partners, offering or securing high-visibility stretch assignments, lobbying for promotions, and so on. The emphasis is on developing a long-term relationship that will continue to evolve as the person's needs and opportunities change.

This is a valuable distinction. For the purposes of this book, I'll use the more familiar term "mentor," but please understand that I am talking about far more than an occasional lunch date to offer friendly advice. A good mentor must have an unequivocal commitment to supporting the mentee over a period of time and lighting a path toward professional development, satisfaction at work, and upward mobility within the organization.

Strong mentor-mentee relationships have a high return for both the individual and the organization. By showing support, and sharing ideas and experiences, mentors reduce the chances of promising female professionals derailing or having their hard work and talent go unrewarded due to political blind spots. Mentors also help both the mentee and the organization by advising on strategic issues such as the selection of new assignments and opportunities, or involvement in international projects, major initiatives, new product development and launch, and so on. For the mentee, a good mentor relationship can provide an enormous boost in confidence, expand professional and organizational knowledge, and offer the assurance of having a trusted go-to person when challenges or difficult decisions arise.

In my firm's work, we emphasize the central importance of having a good mentor. When women do not already have such a relationship, we do what we can to connect them with strategic stakeholders — leaders in the organization who have influence and a good reputation. Consistently we have seen that the right mentor is the tipping point that helps a woman accelerate her career and navigate the organizational terrain with greater confidence and effectiveness. In many cases, the mentor is also the doorway to broader strategic networking, helping the woman to expand her internal and external support system.

In fact, mentoring can help women overcome *many* of the challenges in this chapter. One we haven't talked about yet is "self-promotion." As we'll see when we get to that section, difficulty owning and promoting their abilities and successes is a major obstacle for many women. Whether or not a mentor takes an active role in helping a woman create a personal brand, his or her validation of the mentee's positive attributes and achievements makes it easier for a woman to believe in herself, project a positive image across her strategic network, and trust that the company values her and intends to promote her. The mentor's own promotion of his mentee's accomplishments can also be especially important in impacting the highest levels of management.

Given the power of mentoring in so many different areas, the key phrase for managers is once again: *be proactive*. It's not enough to just be a good mentor — actively work to facilitate strong mentoring relationships for everyone on your team. Start by asking yourself these questions:

- What percentage of your team/department has mentors?
- How many women participate in the mentoring process? Are similar percentages of women and men involved?
- How are you tracking the progress of mentor relationships?
- What is your role in the mentoring process? Are there opportunities to expand that role and better facilitate mentoring relationships?
- Are you "going the extra step" to make sure women have mentoring opportunities and get the full value of the mentoring experience?

Addressing these questions is a reliable way to make sure you are promoting the value of mentoring and facilitating good mentor-mentee matches across your team or department. I can guarantee that better mentoring will mean better individual performance. Just as importantly, a mentor-rich environment fosters better collaboration, teamwork and leadership development.

Don't Ask and You Shall Not Receive

Hard work, competency, and experience are core elements in building career success. But they are not the *only* elements. Other skills and activities must complement those core elements, and become increasingly important in the rise to higher ranks of leadership. My consulting work, and this book, are about paying attention to *all* the elements needed to assure full engagement, development of potential, and achievement — including those that can be especially challenging due to gender or cultural differences.

For example, in today's complex, competitive and fast-changing work environments, women are appreciated for their willingness to take on extra work as it comes. However, research has shown that women are less willing and able to negotiate for the higher pay that should accompany new assignments and expanded roles. They may do an admirable job of asking and negotiating when it comes to their team or clients, but when it comes to personal compensation, they tend to be reticent to ask for what they are really worth.

For many, the aversion to negotiating and asking for what they need is tied to a fear that it will make them vulnerable. When it comes to promotions and stretch assignments, a woman's perfectionist mindset may also restrict her from asking unless she sees herself as a perfect fit. According to an internal Hewlett-Packard study, for example, "women apply for open jobs only if they think they meet 100% of the criteria listed, whereas men respond to the posting if they feel they meet 60% of the requirements."[62]

There is also the female misperception I've touched on before — that "hard work" should stand on its own. As Anna Fels puts it in *Necessary Dreams*, "The idea that merit alone is sufficient is one that women have long cherished. It gives them the rationale for avoiding the 'unfeminine' chore of soliciting support. Unfortunately, there is ample data that high-caliber work, in and of itself, is unlikely to produce appropriate recognition for accomplishments."[63]

Regardless of the cause, "not asking" doesn't just get in the way of individual recognition, the repercussions can also escalate stress, negatively impact well-being and disposition, decrease productivity, and blunt decision-making and innovation. In short, this is not just a personal problem, this is a managerial problem impacting overall business performance.

Gender differences are even more pronounced in negotiating. Ample research shows that, partly due to upbringing, women have a hard time negotiating issues like compensation and career advancement, and are often too quick to compromise. Consider these survey statistics from *Women Don't Ask: Negotiation and the Gender Divide* by Linda Babcock and Sara Laschever:

- 2.5 times more women than men said they feel "a great deal of apprehension" about negotiating.

- Men initiate negotiations about four times more often than women.
- When asked to pick metaphors for negotiations, men picked "winning a ballgame" and a "wrestling match," while women picked "going to the dentist."
- Women will pay as much as $1,353 to avoid negotiating the price of a car, which may help explain why 63% of Saturn car buyers are women.
- Women are more pessimistic about the rewards available, and so come away with less when they do negotiate — on average, 30% less than men.
- 20% of women (22 million people) say they never negotiate at all, even though they recognize negotiation as appropriate and even necessary.[64]

When women cede chances to claim their value, or resign themselves to not receiving the same compensation and opportunities as men, their peers, superiors and society at large tend to follow suit, confirming limiting self-perception and keeping them stagnant. Similarly, it is naïve to think that negotiation is unnecessary — that it's just a matter of time until the world acknowledges your contributions and rewards them fairly. The truth is closer to a saying I often heard in Puerto Rico: If you don't cry you do not eat.

For both individual and organizational performance, it is critical that women develop greater comfort in asking and negotiating for themselves. There are two ways that managers can help. First, openly acknowledge the situation. When you ask why a woman isn't pushing for a promotion or advancement, it encourages her to reflect on the issue — and reinforces the idea that she *should* be pursuing the next step. Second, look at your own structures and processes, particularly when it comes to promotions and compensation. It is hard to develop the self-worth necessary to ask and negotiate more forcefully if you are surrounded by evidence that the company doesn't value women the same as men. Companies need to show that they value and reward talent and effort, regardless of gender. Implementing and promoting a zero tolerance approach to gender pay disparity will not only send a powerful message to individual women in your company, it will also help you attract and retain the best and brightest professionals of both genders.

Going Brandless: Failure to Self-Promote

I've mentioned self-promotion several times in this chapter, but now let's look at it more closely as the last of the nine gender-related challenges I believe every manager and female professional should keep in front of them.

As we learned earlier, physiology and socialization tend to make men seek opportunities to be "one up," to lead, and to win. Self-promotion is a natural extension of that orientation. Women are more inclined to seek rapport, share power and credit, and promote a level playing field. Even when referring to their own work or ideas, they are likely to use the collegial "we" and focus attention on team or departmental performance. For all these reasons, self-promotion does not come naturally. But if women don't *learn* this skill and become comfortable exercising it, they will miss out on opportunities to advance and realize their full potential.

A senior female IT consultant quoted in an article in *The Glass Hammer* puts it this way: "I don't know if it's bravado, arrogance, naïveté, self-delusion or what, but men, no matter how incompetent, pass themselves off as experts. Women tend to be more self-effacing and critical of themselves. Yet, at the end of the day, people believe the story you tell them, period, it's really that simple."[65]

Self-promotion shouldn't be thought of only as making "big" claims often and loudly. It also comes across (or fails to) in subtle ways. Language (ambivalent, tentative words and phrases vs. assertive ones), communication style (indirect vs. direct), tone of voice, body language, and other variables can all make a big difference in whether someone is perceived as a high-performing leader or merely a competent follower.

Many researchers have confirmed this. Deborah Tannen, professor of linguistics at Georgetown University and renowned in academia and the business world, has done extensive work on gender differences in communication. In her well-known book *Talking from 9 to 5*, she explains that women's "conversational rituals...are often ways of maintaining an appearance of equality, taking into account the effect of the exchange on the other person, and expending effort to downplay the speaker's authority so they can get the job done without flexing their muscles in an obvious way." The problem, she adds, is that "when women use conversational strategies designed to avoid appearing boastful and to take the other person's feelings into account, they may be seen as less confident and competent than they really are."[66]

In *Survival of the Savvy*, co-authors Rick Brandon and Marty Seldman mention Tannen's work and identify categories of "weak vocabulary" — tentative, apologetic, self-discounting, ambivalent, and vague — that can undermine how a message is received. While recognizing that there can be strategic reasons to use such phrases, they warn that "weak language usually lowers respect from others, especially more powerful and politically oriented associates. Don't open the door for them to be dismissive or view you as lacking credence and impact." Later, they devote an entire section to "Vocab Rehab" to help readers learn how to present ideas with firm, balanced language.[67]

It is understandable that women struggle with self-promotion. It clashes with the parental voices in their head telling them that nice girls do not show off. But if they listen to those voices, it will severely limit their ability to establish a personal brand, advance through the organization, and self-manage a coherent, satisfying career path. Data shows that people get the career positions they want by advancing on two parallel tracks: competency and internal support. Self-promotion, along with strategic networking and finding a strong mentor, are critical to the latter.

"Competency" itself may be underestimated if a woman is constantly self-demoting rather than self-promoting. The way women speak and carry themselves has a real impact on how their presence is perceived. I saw a good example of this when I was invited to be part of the launch of a women's initiative program at a global corporation whose workforce was predominantly engineers. One participant was a woman who had extraordinary talent, but spoke very softly, sometimes hesitantly, and with a reserved intonation and demeanor. Several of her peers, mostly men, mentioned this to me. The general message was that "she is great at what she does, but she needs to sound like it!"

Women need to develop an authentic, clear voice that allows them to be heard. They also need to be aware that unless they distinguish who is doing the work — "I" not "we" when appropriate — the results they get will not drive the recognition, growth and management positions they deserve.

What can you as a manager do to help women overcome this challenge? There are a number of ways to provide venues and opportunities that will help women become more comfortable asserting a personal brand and developing a narrative about their accomplishments:

- When a female team member does good work, make sure you acknowledge it in a public fashion.
- In meetings and other settings, open up a dialogue that encourages women to talk about the project they did. Prompt them with specific questions about implementation strategies, overcoming challenges that were encountered, and so on.
- Make timely comments to peers and superiors about a female team member's work and talent. Set up meetings (formal or informal) that allow her to tell her story and network with others in the organization.
- If a female team member defers her accomplishments to the team or "we," or if you see someone taking credit for a female team member's idea or work, step in and set the record straight.
- Stop peers from interrupting female team members during a meeting or conversation. Even women who are gaining comfort with self-promotion may not be willing to talk over others to do it. Simply saying, "Let's allow Mary to finish speaking" may give her the space she needs.
- Seek out training and coaching that can help female team members identify areas for growth and improvement, including becoming more assertive, understanding the impact of communication style, etc.

Aversion to self-promotion is another pillar that I see holding up the "glass ceiling." Too often, women give away their intellectual capital and dilute their accomplishments to safeguard a social convention that has little relevance in the business world. It is time for women to learn to blow their own horns — and for managers to reconfigure the corporate conversation to reflect the growing value of women.

Higher engagement and better performance come not from being resigned to a limited, quiet, modest role, but from believing that there is a level playing field that values talent and compensates it accordingly. As a manager, doing what you can to assure that level playing field will give female team members (and foreign nationals who have similar struggles with self-promotion) a much better chance to demonstrate — and even talk about — their full capabilities.

Let me close with an example that I think you will find helpful. On various occasions, my training seminars have involved women from China and Japan — cultures where self-promotion is frowned upon. One particular woman was truly brilliant, respected throughout her organization, and regarded as excellent leadership material by many in top management. When she started our program, she said that she had been offered a position higher in the corporate hierarchy but had turned it down — in part because her mother had advised her to be happy with what she had and not be too ambitious or self-promoting!

However, by declining this position she ultimately put herself and her colleagues in a very unbalanced, unproductive situation. With her superior expertise, the reality was that she did the job of her new boss, yet held the rank, and received the pay, of assistant. Through coaching and strategic training, this fantastic woman became aware that she was not only damaging herself — the *company* could not afford for someone as talented as her to contribute only in a support role. I'm happy to report that changes in her mindset and in the organization eventually elevated her to the leadership role she deserved — and today she is a key member of the top executive team.

CHAPTER 7
Diversity or Adversity?
Cultural Challenges That Impact Performance

In the last chapter we looked at gender-related challenges that companies and managers must address proactively in order to succeed. With today's global workforce, culture-related challenges can be just as difficult and disruptive. There are many overlaps in the challenges that arise due to gender and culture differences, and in the strategies for overcoming them. Indeed, many of my firm's engagements involve addressing both. But in this chapter I will focus on four culture-related issues that stand out in my experience and merit separate attention.

Before getting to specifics, I encourage you to have an open mind, and a healthy dose of skepticism, about your company's existing diversity and inclusion efforts. Almost every large corporation now has diversity programs and messaging in place, typically revolving around "equal opportunities" regardless of origin, gender, ethnic background and sexual orientation. But what is the *reality* of your work environment for those from different cultures? Do they still face obstacles? Are there conflicts and misunderstandings related to their differences?

To build a high-performing 21st century workforce, you can't just claim to be inclusive and celebrate diversity. In fact, such claims can backfire if those outside the dominant culture feel neither included nor celebrated. Regardless of where they come from, people "read" and "feel" the behavior of those around them. If high-minded words and ethically sound policies don't align with day-to-day actions, they will just erode trust, inspire cynicism and undermine performance.

In other words, "we already have a diversity program in place" is not the right mindset. The starting point is to dissect efforts carefully and assess effectiveness. If you're not getting the results you want, you may need to question the entire diversity paradigm you've been working under.

In addition to my consulting work, I teach a university class on Diversity and Ethics, with most of the students being adults from the private sector. What happens in the classroom and workplace is very similar, because we are dealing with fundamentally human challenges here, not just workplace issues. Whether in a classroom or a conference room, the first encounter is always fascinating and reinforces a key point: We can't understand or effectively manage those from other cultures until we understand ourselves and our existing preconceptions. In other words, this isn't just about "them," this is about each of us as individuals. *Self*-assessment is a necessary prerequisite before we move on to talking about the "other."

In a sense, the challenges in this chapter are all failures of vision. They literally involve the individual or organization having "filters" that prevent them from seeing reality clearly, create blind spots, or cause them to see a multi-color world in only one color. "Vision" is also a good analogy in terms of impact. Trying to manage a multicultural workforce without a clear, accurate view of cultural differences is like driving a car while blindfolded. The chances of reaching your destination are slim, and you will undoubtedly have many collisions along the way!

My goal in this chapter is to help you remove the filters, including any "politically correct" lenses prescribed for legal, human resources, or marketing reasons. In my experience, these lenses, although often prescribed with good intentions, can be more compromising than corrective when it comes to the goal of becoming a better, fairer manager and creating an environment where employees from diverse backgrounds can all excel.

Living in Denial:
Failure to Confront Prejudices and Stereotypes

For the past decade, my life and work have revolved almost entirely around improving communication, performance, and opportunities to advance into leadership roles for women and cultural minorities. In this context I've worked with senior executives, HR professionals, frontline managers, and thousands of professionals from diverse cultures. Across the board, one principle is proven again and again: We can't optimize individual and organizational performance just by launching a new initiative, rewriting policies, setting quota-like goals, or spending more on training. All of those may be important, but progress starts with, and ultimately depends on, individual commitment and transformation.

No matter what type of engagement our firm is involved in, the best results come when we are able to help individuals (managers, employees, top executives) challenge and expand their "inner dialogue" regarding who *they* are and how they perceive others. When we inspire someone to enter this process with us, the return on investment is not only better professional performance but also richer personal interactions.

When working with managers, we emphasize that the first step to managing a diverse workforce is to develop a high degree of *self-awareness* about their assumptions and comfort level with "others." In a diverse environment, social interactions inevitably call forth our basic, primal feelings, including prejudices and stereotypes.

As experts in numerous fields have shown, when we meet someone new or different, we instantly create a snapshot of "who they are." Very often that "snapshot" is shaped by unconscious prejudices and stereotypes more than objective knowledge. That makes sense since we don't *have* much objective knowledge when first meeting someone. The problem comes when, instead of getting to know someone better and progressively improving our vision of "who they are," we treat that initial snapshot as the permanent picture. An oversimplified "inner dialogue" about the person and our relation to them then overrides our intellectual capacity to take in new information and develop a more complex and accurate understanding.

Many individuals resist the suggestion that they have prejudices and stereotypes — but we *all* have them. They are a natural legacy of how we are raised, our education and early social interactions, our environmental exposures, and so on. The problem is not "having" them, so much as not being aware of them — and therefore not realizing when they are distorting our perceptions. Obviously, we have to know what our prejudices and stereotypes are before we can try to consciously rise above them.

In the introduction to this chapter, I talked about the gaps that sometimes exist between a corporation's messages of inclusion and diversity and its actions. Similarly, one consequence of not being aware of deeper personal biases and frameworks about "different" people is that there can be a gap between what we say and how we act. You might use all the right words and phrases, but if deep down there is discomfort or lack of appreciation for someone's differences, that will influence your behaviors and decisions — and the "other" will likely "feel" this even if you don't.

So the first cultural challenge to address is not "them" but the values, norms and, yes, stereotypes, that define *our* differences. To explore this effectively, it may help to give yourself permission to acknowledge that some interactions with "others" *are* difficult for you, precisely because they don't fit your "normal" schema and are a different color, have a different accent or physical presence, etc.

Our sense of self and vision of others is strongly influenced by early social interactions. We inherit many beliefs and conceptions from our parents, who inherited them from their parents, back through a chain of generations. Decades ago, that was often sufficient since it was rare to have experiences that went far beyond your family and region. But in a global economy, we can no longer take these beliefs and conceptions for granted. We have to pay attention to how they shape our interactions, who we respect, and why we do or don't do certain things.

The underlying values and experiences of our formative years create what I call the "color" of your soul. To get in touch with this, I often start classes or training engagements by asking participants to close their eyes, envision the color that best represents their values, and then think about why they chose that color. In a group setting, this provides some tangible lessons as everyone takes a turn introducing their color and its meaning. First, every person *has* a color, and the group is comprised of multiple colors — we are *not* "all the same"! Second — what makes our colors unique is that they are tied to personal values, not a team or department or organization. Third, it is possible for the same color to have different meanings — it is very powerful to hear the color one has chosen described differently by someone else!

We all have a color, it is based on personal experiences and values, there are many differences between individuals, and these differences are good — that's *real* diversity! It's also a real start in understanding the "forces" that need to be acknowledged and balanced in order to create a truly inclusive and productive work environment.

I say it's a start — but only a start. Be prepared for obstacles from the old "inner dialogue" regarding how you see and interact with others. Research has shown over and over again that humans have a natural inclination to look for homogeneous environments. People want to feel a sense of control and predictability in social contexts — both personal and professional. Differences can cause us to feel anxious or unsettled, and our response, particularly if we are in a position of power, is often to try to change the "other" to fit *our* ways. Directly or indirectly, we may pressure someone to drop their accent, learn our idioms and communication style and so on.

That's one reason that most corporate cultures are still "white male" environments. Men, mostly of European origin, have dominated individual organizations and the business world in general for ages. They set the dress code, language, behavior, outlook on work and professional development, and other norms — essentially reproducing their own familiar culture in the workplace. Even as the makeup of the workforce has changed, those norms have been passed on. Often the success of the company, its longevity, and presence in markets throughout the world is held up as evidence that this established culture is still working just fine.

However, the multicultural workforce of the 21st century keeps expanding and has reached a critical mass — trying to assimilate everyone into the established environment just won't work anymore. To get back to our color analogy, pretending to have a "colorless" environment isn't credible, and expecting a growing percentage of your workforce to "become" another color or suppress their existing color is unrealistic, and likely to be demoralizing and lead to conflict. One color does *not* fit all — and companies who insist on homogeneity will not be nimble enough to adapt to the new demands of the global economy.

It's part of being human to bring bias and preconceptions to our interactions. But how we *manage* our biases determines whether we can expand the "inner dialogue" to ultimately connect in an honest, effective way with colleagues from other cultures and backgrounds. Doing so is becoming a strategic imperative with bottom-line repercussions. The reality of today's market is that cultural differences must be appreciated and leveraged — not ignored.

All In or Just HR: Who "Owns" Diversity?

Another cultural challenge I see at many companies is that diversity and inclusion are owned almost exclusively by the human resources department. This is *not* in any way to diminish the value of HR. For obvious reasons, HR *is* central to promoting diversity and ensuring that training and policies are aligned appropriately. But unless such efforts are embraced authentically *throughout* the organization, HR activities will have limited success, and those HR wants to help may even perceive efforts as mere tokenism. To succeed, inclusion and diversity must be part of the strategic conversation at the executive leadership level and evident in all areas of operations.

To take an example from my experience, I was once invited to consult with a global company that had been having difficulty with diversity issues. They were growing rapidly and had a strong regional culture, but as they moved into other markets, various problems and misunderstandings arose. The corporate leader I met with had his heart in the right place and was sincerely trying to do his best to eradicate the problems. However, it was clear to me that the thrust of the company's efforts was limited to its training department. "Diversity" was parked at the tactical level, but was not permeating the culture in general. Even small things, like the company website, were not aligned with the stated vision of a more inclusive, culturally sensitive company.

Tactics like mandatory diversity training or sexual harassment training are fine, but how effective can they be if they exist in a vacuum? If you want people to take such training seriously, there needs to be a strategic emphasis on these issues from the C-level down. Likewise, the training needs to be just one part of an integrated strategy that sets the tone for positive change, establishes solid objectives, and monitors progress.

I want to emphasize that the "only in HR" challenge isn't just an issue for companies in the U.S. I have seen this in companies with operations in Europe and Latin America. Most recently, I traveled to Brazil to help launch a diversity and change program for a global company with thousands of employees throughout the world, and once again I was struck by how the ownership of "diversity" rested almost exclusively with HR.

To gain a better real-world understanding of this challenge and a potential direction for solutions, I highly recommend a case study by the Harvard Business School entitled "IBM's Diversity Strategy: Bridging the Workplace and the Marketplace." There is much to learn from this case study, even beyond diversity. To give you just a taste, consider this perspective offered by Lou Gerstner, who became IBM's CEO in 1993. As the case study explains, Gerstner respected IBM's historical commitment to affirmative action and diversity, but felt the company wasn't doing as well as it could in terms of articulating that commitment and bringing it to life. He saw diversity as a strategic issue. His practical viewpoint is a good mindset for any manager in a 21st century corporation:

> "If you took a representative sample of the U.S. population and you put those 100 people in a room, half of them would be women and half of them would be men. And then inside the gender there's roughly 25% ethnic minorities. I just want to get my share of the best people of that 100. When I looked around the room at my executive management team in 1993, we had too many white males among the population, which signaled to me that IBM wasn't getting its share of the talent."[68]

Corporate and Regional Culture: Managing Both Worlds

In the first section of this chapter, we talked about how important it is for individuals, and especially managers, to become aware of their cultural biases and resist the natural tendency to demand homogeneity. The same can be said about your *corporate* culture. Trying to develop a multicultural workforce while clinging rigidly to a "one-color" corporate culture that emerged from a single region is a losing proposition.

That's not to say that "corporate culture" itself is the problem. Far from it — the point is that your corporate culture must evolve to reflect the reality of your workforce and markets. That's a slow process, and along the way it is equally important to leave a little "space" in interactions with those whose native cultural presets are different from the existing corporate culture. Keep in mind that, when dealing with a new culture, it doesn't have to be an either/or absolute — there can be room for "this is how we do it" to co-exist with "that's how you do it." Or to put it on a political spectrum, corporate culture should be an evolving democracy, not a stagnant totalitarian regime.

The core challenge as a company expands into new markets or adapts to the reality of a global workforce is really change management. In fact, thinking about other major change initiatives that have occurred in your organization can give you good insights into how to handle diversity and inclusion efforts.

Any fundamental change in an organization — technology, new leadership, a merger or acquisition, adaptation to market needs, etc. — must be managed. You must overcome people's natural resistance to change, make sure processes are in place for them to learn new information, anticipate likely obstacles, and provide extra support where necessary to help everyone get through the change.

The same is true when bringing a new culture under your corporate umbrella or adapting your corporate culture to be more authentically inclusive. Yet, in every market I visit, when I talk to managers and employees, I usually observe that cultural change is not managed with the same thoroughness and care companies devote to other major changes. We can't expect "diversity" to bloom just because we add the word to the core values in our marketing materials — it takes a lot of work!

Multinational corporations, many of which are publicly traded, face strong legal and ethical imperatives to establish inclusive environments where employees have "equal opportunities" regardless of gender, race, ethnicity, and so on. An environment that is *truly* diverse and inclusive is also a real competitive differentiator, impacting the attraction and retention of top talent, morale and productivity, brand reputation, and more.

Most senior executives understand this — and also that in the global economy "the only constant is change" and they must adapt quickly to new demands and circumstances to succeed, including reaching out to a multicultural workforce.

So what holds these companies back? In organizations where there is a long-term leadership team, it may be their own emotional attachment to the existing culture. Having invested untold time and energy to build the company and establish the strong culture that propelled them to their current level of success, leaders can find it difficult to let go of some aspects of that culture and devote resources to actively change it. Difficult or not, this parallels one of the "stages of decline" Jim Collins warns us about in *Why the Mighty Fall*: "Hubris Born of Success."[69]

The other problem I observe is that diversity and inclusion initiatives keep getting backburnered due to other business priorities. I believe an objective assessment of the current marketplace provides plenty of evidence that understanding and leveraging cultural differences must become a high priority. As the "change framework" outlined in John P. Kotter's *Leading Change* points out, the first step is to create a "higher rate of urgency...in which complacency is virtually absent."[70] That urgency — not just knowing that cultural change is good, but believing that *now* is the moment — is what drives commitment from leadership and employees. If organizational leaders do not convey that sense of urgency and instead settle into the familiarity of an existing corporate culture, the long-term results will be disappointing at best, and could be catastrophic.

Millennials and the New "World Culture"

In Chapter 2, we discussed how generational changes are impacting the workforce. Because Millennials are literally the future of the workforce, I want to end this chapter by looking at some of the unique cultural challenges and opportunities they present.

Due to technology, Millennials in most countries have a different worldview and different attitudes about culture than previous generations. They are more gregarious and naturally inclusive of other cultural viewpoints. The Internet, global media, and expansion and affordability of worldwide travel have made a high percentage of this generation "multicultural" by default. They are less rigidly attached to the cultural presets of their parents and more curious about exploring different ways of life and learning about a broader range of "others." To go back to our color analogy, not only are they receptive to other colors, they may define their own color in terms of a medley of tonalities and hues.

This is refreshing — but there are potential challenges as well. A personal ease with other cultures may lead Millennials to take organization-wide diversity for granted. Corporate initiatives, inclusiveness training and other efforts to consciously create a diverse environment may seem old-fashioned or unneeded. Millennials need to realize that older employees and managers in the organization have not had the same exposures and may have different assumptions and behaviors. As a manager, it is vital to help

Millennials see this big picture — and then leverage their flexibility and amiability toward "others" to help the rest of your team.

A second challenge is that, although Millennials typically have a broad range of cultural exposures and may have friends all over the "cyber-world," the relationships do not always have depth. They may think they understand others better than they do. In particular, those whose relationships are entirely through social media may have blind spots when it comes to real-life workplace interactions. Managers must acknowledge and encourage their natural enthusiasm and sense of connection — yet also direct that energy toward deeper understanding.

Workforce mobility is also reaching new heights with the Millennials. Even companies without multinational operations often have a multinational workforce. An interesting trend for U.S. businesses, however, is that foreign students from this generation do not have the "do anything to stay in the U.S." mindset that was common with previous generations. On the contrary, perhaps partly as a consequence of the post-9/11 response to "non-Americans" in the U.S., many students now leave after graduation.

On one level, it is certainly noble for foreign students to take knowledge and skills gained at U.S. universities and return to help their home countries. But it also represents a drain of young talent. Companies that want to hire the best and brightest Millennials may need to step up recruitment efforts when it comes to foreign nationals. That includes having a corporate culture that "walks the talk" when it comes to inclusion. The last thing you want is to invest time and money in recruiting and hiring talent from other countries, and then have them become so disenchanted with the "one-color" corporate culture that they leave prematurely and take valuable experience and intellectual capital with them.

Bottom line, a company's strategic planning must factor in the very real changes happening in the workforce. You may not have Millennials *on* your leadership team yet, but your leadership team should definitely pay attention *to* Millennials as part of its efforts to create a more inclusive, and productive, workplace environment.

SECTION III
Reflections, Exercises, Tips and Takeaways

Reflections:

- Review the nine gender-related challenges and four cultural challenges in this section. Can you think of real-world examples in your experience that fit these categories?
- Based on what you learned in this section, can you see how misunderstanding an aspect of gender or culture prevented you or another manager from being more effective in a certain situation?
- Almost every wisdom tradition has a variation of the Golden Rule: Do unto others as you would have them do unto you. This simple but profound precept can illuminate common ground with those who seem very different from us. As a manager, how can you apply the Golden Rule, and promote a Golden Rule mindset among team members, when dealing with gender and cultural differences?
- How would you describe your corporate culture? What does it have in common with your cultural background and where does it differ? Do most in your organization naturally embrace the corporate culture? Can you think of areas where it clashes with some individuals' values or upbringing?

Exercises:

- Ask team members to list improvements to make your workplace more gender friendly and culturally inclusive. Have everyone share their ideas, evaluating them in terms of urgency, value and feasibility. Then, as a group, come up with three or four ideas that you can take action on.

- Present some ideas in this section to your team, then ask individuals to write down areas related to gender or culture where they could be more aware and/or improve how they perceive and interact. (You might even add this to your annual review and goal-setting process.) This gives team members and you a common road map based on honest, internal commitment rather than external policies.
- Individually or as a team, identify and dissect a recent workplace problem that involved gender or cultural misunderstandings or conflict. Look at each of the actors involved, their backgrounds, and the forces that contributed to the event going wrong. Then, using knowledge from this section, talk about what everyone could have done better — including systemic or process changes as well as individual perceptions and behaviors.
- Create your own version of the "color" exercise described in Chapter 7. Use it to get your team members to think about their personal "color," where it comes from, and the importance of respecting other people's differences.
- As a group, list as many qualities as you can to describe your existing corporate culture. Discuss differences in individual perceptions. Now make a list describing the *ideal* corporate culture. Establish consensus on key qualities, then discuss actions and strategies to transform your existing state into your ideal state.
- Have your management team and/or female professionals watch and discuss Facebook COO Sheryl Sandberg's TED talk video on "Why We Have Too Few Women Leaders" (www.ted.com/talks/sheryl_sandberg_why_we_have_too _few_women_leaders.html).

Tips:

- *Respond rather than react.* Interactions are more productive when we get out of "reaction mode" — the instinctual, emotional perceptions and behaviors that are driven by the limbic system, amygdalae, and fight-or-flight hormones. In such cases, we bypass or compromise the brain's frontal lobe, where more careful thought and analysis take place. In "response mode" we detach somewhat from our immediate emotions, look at the bigger picture, and consciously choose an appropriate response. While this is good advice for anyone, managers especially should be aware that they may need to take the adult, "response" part of an interaction to de-escalate a reactive situation. The better you are at transforming reactions into responses, the better you can model and teach this behavior as well.

- *Tell the truth about yourself.* Personal honesty and transparency are very powerful in opening a dialogue, helping people connect with you, and generating insights on how to be a better leader. I once had a conversation with a female CEO who was losing too many valued employees. Her partner felt that it was because she was too direct, focusing only on business performance without caring about human issues like job satisfaction. Just minutes before she was leaving to address her corporation's annual kickoff meeting, she asked if I had any advice. Knowing that she had been an entrepreneur from a young age, constantly around men, and had perhaps "overcompensated" to compete, I suggested that she consider contextualizing her message differently when communicating with employees. I advised her to be honest about what drove her personally — then make it clear that her intentions were never to hurt people or scare them away. I also pointed out that some areas of performance, like efficiency, are more meaningful for most employees, so she might focus on those rather than, say, financial projections, which can be confusing and make people feel like they can never do enough. As a follow-up, I later sent this woman some articles. She responded by saying that her kickoff presentation went very well, things were improving, and the advice I'd given her in a few minutes was more transforming than anything

I'd sent her to read. But really, all that advice came down to was "be yourself, but express yourself in a way that shows you are aware of others' needs and expectations as well."

- *Commitment and monitoring must be ongoing.* One mistake I see in terms of workforce gender and culture issues is that there is a big initiative launch, or a new mandatory training regimen, or a flurry of activity to address issues related to a specific incident...and then everything settles back into the status quo. The assumptions and behaviors we're talking about in this book go very deep — you can't change them in a few weeks. There must be an organization-wide commitment to rooting out undesirable behaviors and reinforcing positive behaviors. Also keep in mind that some traditional "reinforcers" may not work as well for women or people from different cultures. Careful monitoring will allow you to make necessary adjustments along the way.

Takeaways:

1. Putting women in a "double bind" is a lose-lose proposition for everyone. It is important to challenge the inner dialogue and misperceptions that create the double bind. Turning the focus from preconceived ideas about how women should or shouldn't act to what is most relevant for work performance will reduce internal and external conflict and stress, and enable women to accelerate career development.

2. Identifying potential "dragon ladies" early and providing appropriate training and coaching can help assertive, competitive women reach their full potential as leaders. One key to such coaching is to help women express strength in ways that, rather than feeling threatening for others, promote positive associations and connections. "Dragon ladies" who are further along in their careers and seem set in their ways may require more targeted, long-term coaching and mentoring with regular check-ins.

3. It is critical for managers to create work environments that invite all team members to participate. A participatory demeanor, tone

and intent on your part will enrich communications and decision-making and have a high payoff in employee morale, productivity and engagement.

4. Preconceived notions and old "internal chatter" can be an obstacle to "hearing" your employees — and to them hearing each other. It is important to override frameworks that may cause us to give some individuals more credibility and attention than others even when they have similar levels of expertise. A good rule of thumb is that if someone is on your team or at the conference table, the assumption should be that they have something to offer and have earned the right to be heard.

5. Some people, especially women, have a hard time delegating because of a fear of failure, mistakes beyond their control, or appearing incompetent by association. However, delegation is absolutely essential to becoming a good leader, so training and professional development must focus on building the "psychological muscle" necessary to delegate effectively.

6. The value of networking should be clearly defined and emphasized as a strategic necessity. There are excellent professionals who specialize in helping companies develop and implement sound networking processes.

SECTION IV — APPLICATION

Creating Gender and Cultural Awareness in the Workplace to Improve Business Performance

I recently worked with a group of multinational companies in Sao Paulo, Brazil. One young male manager told me that any traditional preference for hiring men had to be abandoned because the pipeline of good candidates was increasingly female. "I have 15 headcounts, and 10 are women," he told me. "I have had to learn to accept this reality as my new normal."

The "new normal" in business is that women will continue to enter the workforce in higher numbers than men in almost every country. Similarly, *global* business interactions are becoming the rule rather than exception. Even companies that don't actively operate or compete in international markets (yet) will continue to see greater diversity in their workforce, supply chains, and strategic relationships, including outsourcing partners.

In short, the answer to the question posed by the title of this book is unequivocally "No!" Companies *cannot* afford to ignore women or people from different cultures. Creating better gender and cultural awareness and interaction in the workplace is not just a "good" thing to do — it's becoming a competitive necessity.

Most companies and individual managers grasp this and are making some effort to understand and address gender and culture issues — but results are not always living up to expectations. Committing to the effort *is* a necessary (and admirable) first step! But efforts may need refining or expert guidance to be fully effective.

As I point out before starting a new consulting engagement, there are no "instant solutions" when it comes to gender and cultural differences. We need to take a step back and look at the big picture, then commit to an ongoing journey that will be about self-transformation as well as organizational change.

The structure and content of this book embody that approach. We started by looking at the historical context and social trends that have shaped the modern workplace. Next we discussed physiological and societal forces that impact our perceptions, behaviors and interactions. Then, having established that fundamental knowledge, we honed in on specific types of gender and culture challenges that arise in most workplaces and undermine performance.

Throughout I have provided tips and advice from my own experience to help managers respond to the challenges. But now let's take the gender and culture intelligence we've developed and apply it in the more focused context of assembling and managing teams.

In Chapter 8, I'll explore top-level approaches to help you tap the benefits of gender-balanced, multicultural teams, proactively remove obstacles, and cultivate environments where diverse individuals can excel — and excel together. Chapter 9 will cover management strategies that are especially important due to the increasing reliance on "virtual teams," including five bridge-building approaches that I believe every manager should understand and regularly employ.

The "bridge" analogy is one I've used throughout *Can You Afford to Ignore Me?* I cannot emphasize enough how valuable senior executives and managers can be in this role. The gender and cultural differences in today's business world are not going away — nor should we want them to go away! Harnessing complementary synergies presents rich opportunities to raise business performance to new levels. But someone has to engineer and build the bridges that connect individuals who have traditionally been disconnected. At your organization, that someone is you!

CHAPTER 8
Unleashing the Power of Balanced Teams

Teams have become the default organization structure for most companies. Almost every manager and employee, especially at large organizations, regularly works within, or has been intensely involved with, teams and team-centered projects. The team approach has many potential benefits, including reduction of downtime and implementation, better knowledge transfer, increased creativity and innovation, reinforcement of the drive for excellence, and more.

Unfortunately, as we hear from many of our clients, realizing those benefits can be challenging. Differences in culture, communication style, and so on can complicate the management of teams. Almost everyone reading this book can probably relate an experience, either as a manager or as a team member, where a team was being pulled in so many different directions that it could never move forward!

In this chapter, I want to offer some suggestions to help you overcome team building and team management challenges with respect to gender and cultural differences. And the first suggestion is that we need to see that diversity on teams is not a problem — it's a solution.

Findings by Claremont Graduate University's Paul Zak, a pioneer in the field of neuroeconomics, raise the possibility that teams, as social networks, may stimulate the production of oxytocin. As you may recall from Chapter 3, oxytocin is a hormone that correlates to feelings like trust, empathy and generosity. Zak calls it a "social glue" and "economic lubricant."[71]

Whether or not teams, simply by their nature, actually increase feelings of belonging and trust, those feelings *are* necessary for good team performance. That reinforces the value of good gender and culture balance on teams. For example, consider the fact that women *naturally* produce higher levels of oxytocin, even when subjected to stress, while difficult situations tend to reduce oxytocin and boost stress hormones for men.

That's just one physiological example of how the presence of women can bring balance to a team and improve overall performance.

Numerous researchers have explored this topic, but I want to call out one group of researchers in particular for stimulating my own thinking in this section of the book: Anita Woolley, Thomas Malone, Christopher Chabris, Sandy Pentland and Nada Hashmi. If you want to explore their work, you can get a good overview by reading the interview, "Defend Your Research: What Makes a Team Smarter? More Women" published in the June 2011 *Harvard Business Review*.

I think you will find that turning our focus toward teams will help you connect the dots between the various topics we've covered in the first three sections of this book. As we've seen, physiology, socialization, culture, and historical and societal trends all have a profound influence on behaviors that help or hinder team performance depending on how they are managed. That awareness is a big first step — the next step is to consider how to *apply* this new knowledge in practical ways.

Gender and cultural balance help teams deliver the strategic benefits mentioned at the start of this chapter. When talented people with diverse views and approaches work in a unified, strategic fashion, the results will far surpass the "group think" of homogeneous teams or the underperformance that inevitably happens when there is constant conflict and misunderstanding. In the global economy, smart team-building that leverages different talents, personal qualities, knowledge, and experience across culture and gender may be the difference between your company's — and your own — failure or success.

Let's stop losing sleep worrying about gender and cultural differences — and begin exploring how those differences can be key elements in creating high-performing teams. Welcome to the 21st century — and may the best teams win!

Begin With Balance: A Strategic View of Team Composition

Understanding that physiological, social and cultural factors all create tendencies toward certain emotions and behaviors is a powerful tool for managers, because it gives you insights on how to strategically balance the composition of your teams. However, when we say "balance," we don't mean just make sure to add at least one woman or team member from another culture.

In fact, experts have found that when teams include only a small percentage of people who are of a different gender or cultural background, overall team performance rarely reaches desired levels and may be poor. This is partly because, whether intentional or not, it can evoke feelings of tokenism that become a demoralizing emotional contagion.

Another issue, particularly in environments where differences are suppressed rather than embraced, is what some researchers call "interpersonal congruence," or "the degree to which group members see others in the group as others see themselves." For example, research by Hillary Elfenbein and Jeffrey Polzer, reported in the article "Identity Issues in Teams", found that "diversity tended to improve creative task performance in groups with high interpersonal congruence, whereas diversity undermined the performance of groups with low interpersonal congruence."[72]

In other words, when team members have an accurate understanding and appreciation of individual differences, including those related to gender and culture, the team performs better. When team members see inaccurate stereotypes of each other or pretend that everyone is the same, performance suffers. We all want to be seen accurately and known for who we really are, and we are better able to communicate, interact and respond to one another when our relationships are based in authenticity. *That's* interpersonal congruence — and without it, the chances of developing high-performing, or even productive, teams are slim.

Tokenism, interpersonal incongruence, and inconsistent standards can all make visible minorities on a team feel like they have to talk more to be heard and do twice as much to get half the credit. In such an environment, is it any surprise that many would become burned out, emotionally fatigued or frayed, or disengaged?

The *Harvard Business Review's* "Two Women, Three Men on a Raft" article and subsequent commentary also remind us that a minority may be actively undermined by a majority. The article, a classic in analyzing how gender dynamics can impact leadership and performance, showed that the women involved fell short in leadership roles because the men on their team consistently engaged in behaviors that created challenges and uncertainty. In a sense, the women just gave up.[73] If you recall what we learned in Section II, this can be attributed in some ways to how men are wired — they instinctually needed to protect territory, own the process, and prove they could "win."

Such scenarios have a pernicious side effect beyond immediate performance: They reinforce existing misconceptions that adding a woman or minority to a team will just create problems. So, again, simply adding a couple different faces is not the same as creating a balanced, high-performing team. The latter requires careful thought during the selection process to avoid tokenism, and proactive effort throughout the team's life span to curtail the challenges I've just mentioned.

In this sense, "team composition" isn't just about who is on the team, it's also about context and expectations — the playing field where the team will perform. Here are a few managerial solutions to ensure that your team functions in an optimal fashion:

- Set the right expectations and tone from the start. Explain why diverse teams can achieve more if they work together effectively, then emphasize that fairness, respect, openness to collaboration, and valuing different viewpoints are critical to what the team needs to accomplish.
- Communicate the strategic importance of full engagement and contributions from every team member — which also means making sure there is space for everyone to contribute.
- As you're forming the team, and throughout the project, identify potential challenges related to gender and cultural differences, and be ready to step in and reframe perceptions and behaviors for specific individuals. Be clear that you're not asking anyone to give up traits that come naturally, but that conscious self-regulation of those traits is sometimes important for both individual and team success.
- Before getting into the project itself, do some simple exercises to help get stereotypes and prejudices out in the open. I consistently observe a great sense of relief as people realize it's okay to look at each other's differences. The resulting self-awareness — and other-awareness — make it easier to identify and remove obstacles and achieve

the high level of interpersonal congruence necessary for optimal performance.

- Seek ways to build and reinforce trust among team members. Conversely, if you see miscommunication or misunderstanding undermining trust, step in quickly to "bridge" differences.
- Training and coaching are excellent tools — remember that they are highly effective when it comes to personal challenges that prevent better communication, team building, leadership and performance.

Addressing all aspects of "team composition" to ensure balance may require a bit more work upfront, but the payoff can be huge. Remember, women and those from other cultures add complementary value that you're unlikely to get from a homogeneous or all-male team. For example, most women *like* collaborative environments — and have qualities that are assets to team performance, including a natural inclination toward mutual support, give-and-take, multi-tasking and "big picture" thinking.

"Innovative Potential: Men and Women in Teams", a fascinating study by Lynda Gratton, Elisabeth Kelan, Andreas Voigt, Lamia Walker and Hans-Joachim Wolfram, offers some interesting insights in this regard. Published by the London Business School in 2007, it found that many qualities affecting team performance peak when there is a 50-50 gender mix, including "psychological safety," "experimentation" and "efficiency." Interestingly, "self-confidence" peaked when females had a slight 60-40 majority.[74]

Bottom line, becoming adept at creating and managing teams that have a balance of gender and multicultural qualities will give your company — and you — a huge competitive advantage moving into the future.

Balancing Teams by Type and Purpose

Balancing a team's composition depends on its type and purpose. That varies across industries, companies, and projects, and will include variables that only you as manager will know for a given team. However, let's take a brief look at three well-known, top-level team types to illustrate how gender and cultural intelligence can help you optimize performance by matching different skills and personal qualities with each team's mission and needs. These three types are referenced in many sources and texts, including *Management* by Stephen Robbins and Mary Coulter.

As you read, keep in mind that adjustments to your "normal model" are often necessary when doing business in other countries or managing team members from diverse cultures. For example, in some cultures, clear rules and lines of authority are desired regardless of the type of team, while cultures like the U.S. tend to prefer a higher degree of latitude and self-management. So, approach these team types as basic templates rather than rigid, fully defined structures. Our discussion here is meant to get you thinking about areas for each team type that may need attention, not to prescribe specific adjustments.

Self-Managed Teams

Self-managed teams typically involve about eight to 15 team members. They are often permanent and have key ongoing responsibilities such as:

- Set pace and urgency of work
- Define tasks and farm out work to appropriately skilled or specialized resources
- Select and fire members
- Coordinate scheduling, including vacations
- Choose a leader (often this position rotates)

As the name implies, these teams have a high degree of autonomy. They usually have a fairly democratic structure, and collaboration and coordination between team members is important. At the same time, there must be a strong leader to provide direction and help the team maintain momentum and stay on track. Such a leader must be able to read people well, make tough decisions and bridge any gaps that arise between team members.

Because a self-managed team will operate autonomously, it is important at the outset to clearly articulate expectations, set a tone for how the team should function, and define successful outcomes. Gender and cultural awareness is particularly important, especially for anyone chosen as a leader. Potential conflicts or gaps should be addressed proactively. For example, if a woman is chosen leader for a team with members from cultures where males are traditionally dominant (such as the Middle East), you will want to meet with the woman to alert her to the level of "pushback" she may experience and give her tips for handling it. Similarly, you would also want to meet with those from the male-dominated cultures to emphasize that cooperation and collaboration with the female leader is strategically important for them, the team and the company. From personal experience, I know that it is possible for team members in such a scenario to learn to work together effectively — but it requires patience, commitment, and some gender-smart, culture-smart guidance!

Problem-Solving Teams

Problem-solving teams are typically formed to define new solutions and opportunities for improvement. Their role is to think through problems and processes and make suggestions, not to implement changes. You want good communicators on such a team, both to ensure dynamic, idea-generating interactions among team members and to provide a clear presentation of good news, bad news, and recommendations to stakeholders.

Gender and cultural diversity is extremely valuable on these teams, since effective problem-solving depends on getting many different perspectives. The projects these teams are assigned often require thinking outside the box, exploring "what ifs," and pushing to do what hasn't been done before. Homogeneous groups cannot do this effectively. If your teams aren't achieving the results you need and expect, it may be time to take a look at how they are configured.

The challenge is not just to have diverse team composition, but to be sure the environment encourages full engagement and expression — these teams can't afford to ignore anyone! To get the most out of diversity, it is also important to have coherent processes, anticipate possible communication gaps, and establish unifying goals and parameters to keep the team on track.

Cross-Functional Project Teams

Some projects or events require assembling professionals from different functions, departments and operating entities within an organization. Such teams have a limited life span, and can present numerous challenges that must be resolved to succeed. Besides gender and cultural diversity, these teams add a layer of "professional" diversity that brings the potential for misunderstanding and conflict. People from different professions or disciplines may not speak the same "language" about business and may have different ways of thinking and communicating. Unless goals and processes are clearly defined, you may end up with team members moving in opposing directions.

Other challenges arise when cross-functional project teams require specialists or knowledge workers who do not normally work in teams. As experts who know they are good at what they do, they may have a tendency to hold their ground, be more rigid about information-sharing, or resist efforts to establish a sense of congruence at the team level.

As a representative of a U.S.-based company, I once had to assemble a team of directors to launch a huge marketing program for a home appliance manufacturer in Mexico. I met with the marketing team, procurement team, quality control team and manufacturing plant team to try to get everyone on the same page before launching the initiative. As you can imagine, each group wanted the process predicated on their own perceptions and business discipline. Marketing wanted a strategy to fit their framework, quality control wanted to pursue a more conservative and time-consuming route, procurement wanted to expedite the process to work with their timetables and production requirements, and so on.

I put many lessons from this book into practice during this engagement! As a woman, I knew I would be perceived as collaborative rather than competitive, and I made full use of that perception to build consensus between the highly charged powerhouses I worked with from each business unit. By remaining aware of their gender and cultural expectations and assumptions, I was able to manage communications to avoid unnecessary conflicts and keep us moving toward the goal. Being from a U.S. company made me an outsider, so I took extra measures to show respect and sensitivity. I emphasized that the U.S. corporation was interested in a long-term business relationship to help offset potentially negative preconceptions that some team members may have had. I also leveraged the similarities in our cultural backgrounds and took the time to build personal relationships within this close-knit network.

I put a *lot* of effort into showing and encouraging empathy and establishing a high degree of congruence among this team's members. My days were long, with uncountable meetings, business lunches, and late dinners, but the invested time and relationship-building paid off. In the end, the team functioned *as* a team and was able to successfully develop, manufacture and market a distinctive new product line.

Clearly Define Roles and Communication Paths

Multicultural teams require you to be on the lookout for differences in how people perceive concepts like power, individualism and success. Today's technology has made it easy to connect team members around the world — but it hasn't changed the fact that different cultures often have real differences in values, ways of thinking, and basic assumptions about business. If we don't take time to understand these differences, align perceptions and make sure everyone is treated respectfully, technology will connect us to conflict rather than the benefits of a diverse workforce.

Some differences are readily apparent, such as opposite viewpoints and reactions to authority. Other differences, such as concepts related to "time," can be dangerously easy to overlook. Make no mistake, serious inefficiency and discord can arise from basic country-to-country differences related to appropriate turnaround times, feelings about responsiveness, ways of signifying urgency, and the rigidity or malleability of schedules.

One good way to avoid problems related to such differences is to clearly define roles, tasks, measures for accountability, and communication paths right from the start. Helping your team develop a shared understanding of basic expectations and responsibilities provides a firm foundation for interactions. Even if misunderstandings occur later in the process, that foundation can make it easier to work things out.

Language barriers can undermine even the best efforts to address differences and establish clear roles and processes, so I recommend that, whenever possible, team members all be able to communicate fluently with each other in one common language. "Fluently" is a key word — do not assume that if someone speaks a language, they are fluent. Also, encourage all team members to avoid idiosyncrasies and slang that may be specific to one region.

As someone from a Latino culture who works with people from many different countries, I am very sensitive to language issues — but also living proof of how easy it is to slip and use a phrase that causes confusion. I was recently introduced to a new professor from Greece at the university where I teach as adjunct faculty. As we were exchanging pleasantries, I used the phrase "sink or swim" — which prompted a quizzical look and a question about what I meant. I had overlooked the possibility that, while common in the U.S., that expression might be completely foreign to someone who learned English in another country.

Keep in mind that cultures also have different styles and protocols for body language, phone and email, proper meeting conduct, and so on. Some cultures, for example, have a more formal approach to meetings, including phone meetings, in terms of who leads and when others should feel comfortable voicing ideas. Email practices vary widely, as do feelings about the appropriateness of communicating via texting. With so much room for misunderstanding and confusion, you can see why it is critical to nail down basics like roles and responsibilities, and why you should encourage team members to not take *any* aspect or mode of communication for granted.

Set the Tone for Successful Female Presence and Diversity

Throughout this book, I've shown that, beyond humanistic and ethical concerns, there is a strong business case for adding diversity to your teams and making sure women and people from other cultures have opportunities to contribute fully. "Is There a Payoff From Top-Team Diversity?" — the April 2012 *McKinsey Quarterly* article cited in Section III — is one of many publications in recent years to answer that question with a resounding, statistically based "Yes!" Companies can't afford to ignore this data any more than they can afford to ignore the availability of new technology in their industry, shifts in market demands, or other critical strategic developments.

For many companies my consulting firm works with, the problem isn't that they're ignoring the trend. They're trying to get more women and cultural diversity into their leadership pipeline. Diversity is an explicit or implicit goal driving their recruiting, training, professional development and other programs. And yet — they're struggling to achieve their goals, talented individuals continue to derail, and workforce conflicts continue to be common.

Why? Often, we need to get out of the executive offices and move closer to the ground level of the organization to find the problems — and solutions. Clearly, I believe in the power of training and coaching to help improve an individual's chances of succeeding, but that alone will not get companies where they want to be. We also have to build a foundation for success from the ground up. Top management must understand how entry-level and mid-level employees perceive gender and culture-related issues. Those employees are key to creating a balanced work environment, and they will respond if they feel that top management "gets it," has put appropriate mechanisms in place, and is articulating a clear, compelling narrative around the organization's long-term commitment to diversity.

Efforts to overcome gender and culture challenges must go deeper than integrating the word "diversity" into the corporate mission and adding an hour of mandatory diversity training to the calendar — because the challenges themselves go to the most fundamental level of our perceptions.

For example, consider the results of an experiment that Stanford University professor Frank Flynn conducted with one of his business classes. He took a *Harvard Business Review* case study showing how Heidi Roizen had leveraged networking and self-promotion to become a successful executive, venture capitalist and entrepreneur. With Harvard's permission, Flynn made a second version of the case study where the only change was that "Heidi" became "Howard." Each class member then did an online evaluation of the case study's subject covering multiple dimensions. As Flynn recounts, "students were much harsher on Heidi than on Howard across the board. Although they think she's just as competent and effective as Howard, they don't like her, they wouldn't hire her, and they wouldn't want to work with her."[75]

As a manager, you must defuse the impact of such prejudices, or any "Heidi" on your team will never reach her full potential — indeed, the team itself will never reach *its* full potential!

Managers like you are really the central link between a company's "good intentions" regarding gender and cultural diversity and an environment where individual and team performance can truly excel. Here are some suggestions that will help you integrate your talent and ensure that everyone can make a significant contribution to the team:

- **Check power dynamics**. Remember, there is a natural physiological and sociological tendency for most women to seek balance, collaborate, and embrace a more democratic approach to participation and acknowledgement. That should be an asset, but pay attention to the structure and tone of meetings to make sure "democratic" voices aren't constantly outshouted and shut down.

- **Build trust**. As pointed out in the introduction to this chapter, trust is essential to team performance. Opening up time for socializing and befriending so that everyone can get the "feeling" of the group has a high payoff in general, and is especially important for women or those who feel like cultural "outsiders." One-on-one meetings and group exercises will enable the team to develop a sense of connection before they start tackling work challenges.
- **Provide clear direction and leave space for questions**. All team members benefit when goals, processes and expectations are clearly spelled out in advance. It is equally important, especially with a multicultural workforce, to allow space for questions to ensure that everything is fully understood. Remember that questioning, including "why" and "what if" questions that may arise around a directive, is a natural part of a woman's communication process. If it becomes excessive, coaching to self-regulate and break free of the "perfection syndrome" may be advisable. But in general, the extra questions will benefit the entire group, often turning up issues that others overlooked or that weren't obvious in the short term but could cause problems later. Brooksley Born again comes to mind — she raised the right questions to address what turned out to be an enormous risk for our economy, but because the economy was performing well short term, her questions were ignored.
- **Coach good listening**. Some team members, particularly men, may be impatient with the extra listening and consideration of different viewpoints required with a more diverse team. Be proactive in explaining the value of active listening, questioning, and integrating a range of perspectives. If you want contributions from all team members, it

must be clear that such contributions are desired, respected and valued.

- **Choose the right leaders**. The skills and qualities required to successfully lead a diverse team are different than those that work with homogeneous teams. Intellectual competency and experience in a particular field are important, but so is the ability to develop a sense of commonality and congruence. Before putting people in leadership roles, make sure they are comfortable in their skin, self-aware, gender-smart and culturally sensitive, and that they have both emotional intelligence and bandwidth.

- **Bring in and support "newcomers."** You won't achieve diversity or help professionals grow by bowing to group or individual pressure to assemble teams where everyone already knows each other and shares a similar background. Keep the focus on what the team must accomplish, and emphasize the unique skills and qualities that newcomers will add. You can also point out the downsides of "group think" and that new faces and voices will help everyone gain a fresh perspective. Particularly if newcomers are in the minority, be sensitive to the fact that you, and other team members, may need to reach out more actively to help them "fit in" and develop productive relationships.

- **Don't let competitiveness result in a losing team**. Some individuals and corporate cultures embrace a kind of competitiveness that can undermine group performance, particularly when a group involves women or people from high-context communication cultures. Emphasize that *team* success is paramount and undermining others to advance a personal agenda won't be tolerated. The way you frame and reward collaboration and competition (is the project about the "I" or the "we") will greatly influence individual and team performance. Create a contextual and psychological environment that supports and integrates contributions from all members. Don't allow "raw competition" to elevate one or two individuals but destroy the team.

Provide Support Through All Phases of Team-Building

Many corporate team-building processes are based on a four-step model first created by Bruce Tuckman in 1965: forming; storming; norming; performing. Whether your organization uses those exact words or not, the steps probably parallel yours, so let's use this model to examine the manager's role and areas of gender and culture that merit attention in each. An important point is that gender and cultural challenges must be considered *throughout* the process, not just at the start. There are always judgment calls to make about when to step in and when to let individuals or a team learn by trial and error; however, with gender and culture issues, you may want to err on the side of intervention. Because of prejudices, misconceptions and misunderstandings, you can easily have a team that is stuck or failing and doesn't even realize it!

Forming

The initial phase of team building is critical in creating a gender-balanced, culturally diverse team that will perform to its full potential. I have devoted whole sections of this chapter to team composition, defining roles, and "setting the tone," but some points bear further emphasis. If a team gets off to a solid start and individual team members have a clear idea of objectives, develop a good rapport, and share an understanding of what success will look like and how they'll get there, then there is a good chance they'll be able to work through the challenges they encounter along the way. Conversely, if a team is "malformed" from the start, it can be difficult to get things "in shape" during later phases.

One important message to give to your diverse team as they enter this phase is that different views are valuable and certain kinds of "conflict" should not only be expected, but embraced! At the same time, this is the phase where you need to build those first bridges across gender and culture gaps and make it clear that respectful collaboration and integration of multiple perspectives is a must for team performance.

I use various tools to support teams in this phase, from individual coaching to full-scale training seminars. Exercises that open a dialogue contrasting our "inner voice" with outside perceptions are particularly valuable. Asking team members to describe personal attributes and share them as a group is a powerful way to get everyone to reflect on their own uniqueness while becoming more aware and respectful of the uniqueness of others. This creates an experiential "baseline" where appreciation of differences trumps expectations of assimilation, and encourages everyone to begin considering how individual differences can blend together in the big picture.

Such exercises work best in person — I always recommend that at least part of the forming phase involve face-to-face contact if possible. Technological solutions that evoke a face-to-face experience — such as Skype, teleconferencing, videoconferencing, and internal websites that allow video exchange — are the second best option, but may fall short in many situations.

Many managers I've known echo the sentiments recently expressed to me by a manager with reports in multiple Latin American countries. During a training-related discussion about keeping people engaged and committed, he said he had attempted to use technology in various contexts, but it did not yield effective results compared to having in-person meetings. His solution was to visit each market once a month to spend a full day with each team or individual. He added that this approach was especially important in the first stage of team-building.

Typically, the role of a manager during this phase is to help define a schema of work, and point the way toward basic objectives, but not necessarily to dictate every detail. If you think about some of the gender and cultural differences we've discussed, you will see that this is a critical time to facilitate a team dialogue — which may include encouraging some members to speak up and others to become better listeners. The strongest teams tend to be those where a rich exchange of ideas and information yields real consensus on the team's purpose and goals — sometimes referred to as the team's "charter." The groundwork for such an exchange happens during the forming phase.

Storming

The storming phase is where the team actively hashes out different ideas and possibilities on everything from defining the primary problem to be solved to leadership models and how to move forward. Understandably, this can be unsettling and provoke conflicts. Some teams even stall at this stage and wither away without accomplishing anything.

Many women, as well as team members from high-context or large power distance cultures, may be averse to conflict and compromise their views or shut down if there is not strong support (or authoritative "permission") from a manager to voice their concerns. It can be tempting to sweep differences under the rug, but a better strategy is to use these moments to promote deeper, more dynamic communication among team members. Short term, you want a high degree of engagement and the decision-making benefits that come when multiple perspectives weigh in. Longer term, if you can get people comfortable with this level of exchange, even when it feels contentious, they will be able to continue communicating at that level throughout the team's life span — a huge plus.

To increase comfort levels and ensure participation, it may help during this phase to ask team members to first define issues as individuals, then facilitate a meeting to share and debate issues, raise and answer questions and objections, and shepherd the team through the process of aligning and converging. As issues are debated, keep in mind that some team members may be less naturally vocal or assertive than others. You may want to intervene, subtly or more directly, in order to "push" good ideas forward. Sometimes getting a better balance is as simple as asking for it — if you notice that someone hasn't been heard, take the initiative and ask "what is your viewpoint on this issue?"

Norming

In this phase, everything is settling into place. Having started with a diverse group of individuals, you should now have a more established team mentality. (Research suggests that the presence of women or people from cultures that naturally think in terms of "we" instead of "I" tends to allow this to happen more easily.) The team has defined and agreed on basic processes and responsibilities, communication paths, and so on.

Should you just sit back and assume everything will go smoothly? Never — and especially not when there is the threat of misperceptions or miscommunication due to gender or cultural differences. Yes, the team should now have a solid direction and operational momentum, and you should take a step back. But as someone outside day-to-day operations, you have a singularly valuable ability to spot and respond to issues that may threaten interpersonal congruence or team unity. Remain vigilant!

Performing

When a team reaches this phase, it should essentially be self-sufficient and require little or no direction from a manager in order to complete projects, make decisions, and resolve internal conflicts.

However, I want to highlight two ongoing managerial roles that are especially important for gender-balanced, multicultural teams. First, remember that women and people from certain cultures may find it difficult to self-promote. As a manager you're in a great position to lead by example and praise excellent work both directly and to others throughout the organization. Show your commitment to promoting the team and its individual members, and, where necessary, coach individuals in how to network, enhance their presence, and strengthen their personal brand. Celebrating achievement is good for men and women of every culture!

Second, particularly with teams that function over long periods of time, remember that change is a constant. Tuckman's model recognizes that teams can fluctuate between phases. For example, a team that has reached the performing phase may revert to the storming phase after a leadership change, addition of new team members, or shifts in responsibilities due to strategic or operational changes at the company. Managers should anticipate these fluctuations — which could also happen due to shifting gender or culture dynamics — and adapt their level of participation accordingly.

Manage Multinational Teams, Don't Colonize Them

Can team-building processes and management styles that work well in your U.S.-based company be applied to a more diverse, multinational team? Yes and no.

Yes, methodologies like Tuckman's four-phase model provide a good structural basis for team-building in almost any location, while leaving space to adapt details to a specific team composition or project. And yes, as a "parent" company you have the right to pass on your corporate culture and values and encourage new employees, wherever they may be, to embrace and uphold "who we are" as a company.

But no, it will not be effective to insist that a new culture or foreign nationals must do everything *exactly* like your U.S. employees. There is a big difference between encouraging someone to find their place in your culture and dictating that they must abandon all their natural values and behaviors — or else. When you do the latter, you're bound to inspire resistance, deflate morale — and miss out on differences that could expand and strengthen your culture.

The best approach is what some people call "globalocal" — being simultaneously aware of, and making a conscious effort to balance, "global" and "local" realities. I'll talk more about this in terms of corporate culture in the next section. Here I want to emphasize that a little sensitivity to "local" cultural issues can go a long way. Issues that may seem insignificant within your cultural mindset may be extremely impacting for foreign nationals. A simple example I see many U.S. companies struggle with is holidays. The calendar is big enough to schedule meetings and deadlines without imposing upon the major holidays of *anyone* on the team. When U.S. holidays are respected and others are ignored, it yields frustration, resentment and unnecessary logistical challenges.

I have been personally impacted by this on numerous occasions, including a project I coordinated in Latin America through a major U.S. academic institution. Although the Latin American company's request for proposal came at the beginning of summer, the university took more than four weeks to finalize approval of my proposed scope of work. That pushed us into July, a month that most people in Latin America (and Europe) are on vacation. As a result, the client had a hard time reaching key stakeholders to get approval and buy-in for the project, causing further delays. This project was strategically urgent for the company — and greater awareness of the Latin American vacation schedule among university personnel could have saved everyone a lot of stress.

The takeaway here is that it's important to equip yourself and other team members with as much information as possible so that everyone understands cultural and regional issues that may need to be taken into consideration. That extends to behavior styles as well — a fundamental source of contention in the engagement that catalyzed my desire to write *Can You Afford to Ignore Me?* As you may recall from the introduction to this book, I had been invited to talk to a multinational pharmaceutical company about the special attributes that Latina women bring to the workforce. But the comments I heard from the women themselves were very impacting. Many said they felt "forced to do things 'the American way' all the time" and that "there is little space for our way of thinking and communication style."

One woman that I spoke with at length was a chemical engineer who had been with the company since graduating from college. She loved her work and had accumulated significant institutional knowledge, but was considering leaving because she felt "stuck." Specifically, she said she felt excluded, unheard and constantly challenged when she had to participate in planning team meetings.

As we talked, I realized that a root cause of her frustration involved communication style. She said that men on her team constantly told her she was too passionate and intense, that her high level of energy was "overwhelming." Two issues jumped out at me then, and they are important lessons when managing a multicultural team. First, although this woman was constantly criticized, no one had given her constructive feedback or coaching about how to self-regulate or modify her style to fit her audience. Second, there was no managerial intervention to help team members learn to understand her communication style and focus on the valuable content rather than the form of delivery. There was no middle ground — the expectation was that the Latina woman must communicate like them or be silent.

This attitude has been the norm in many companies for decades: Our company has hired you, so change to our way of doing things and suppress your differences. Assimilate, assimilate, assimilate. This paradigm was never truly effective, but in the past many felt it was the only option and did their best to endure assimilation.

However, today's global marketplace is very different. Multinational companies — and career opportunities — are not limited to those with U.S. or European headquarters. And top companies, regardless of home base, have recognized that diversity, not assimilation, is the path to greater productivity and organizational excellence. Talented professionals have choices and won't stick around environments where they must abandon their culture and authentic qualities as individuals. To compete as a multinational, you must manage with multinational sensitivity.

Bridging Corporate Culture and Local Office Culture

Before getting to specific tips on matching your management style to different cultural orientations, I want to take a closer look at one more way that managers form an important "bridge" for team members: connecting corporate and local office cultures.

In a sense this is an extension of the "globalocal" approach discussed in the last section, but it is an easy area to overlook. Focused on obviously visible differences of nationality, language, and so on, even culturally sensitive managers may lose sight of gaps between the corporate and local office cultures that should also be addressed.

Corporate culture is the overarching contextual structure that tells the world who your company is, what it values, and how it operates. It may include sophisticated brand identity guidelines, dress codes, characteristics of the physical workplace, philosophical approaches to compensation and professional development, relations with local communities, philanthropic efforts, and much more. If a company is predominantly located, or has a long history, in one country or region, there is a good chance the corporate culture will include aspects of that culture as well.

When expanding into new markets and managing multinational teams, corporate culture can be a useful, unifying structure. Being able to clearly articulate the qualities that make your company unique provides the same kind of stability, guidance, and sense of belonging that comes from any other type of culture. When this is done right, new employees can more quickly find where they fit in to the big picture — and add their unique qualities to *expand* that big picture.

However, just as you have to strike a balance to respect and integrate, rather than assimilate, individual cultural differences, it's important to recognize that local offices will have their own way of doing things and business norms that may not perfectly align with how you do it back at headquarters. When your company opens a new office in another country, for example, you will probably find that the locals have their own established protocols and practices when it comes to communicating, work-life balance, vacations, meetings, and so on. Aspects of the local culture will also inevitably influence how people relate to each other and set the tone for how work gets done. This complete microcosm existed before your company arrived — and it won't disappear just because you project a new corporate macrocosm into the space.

Managers have a valuable role in bridging the differences between these two environments. You must decide how to create a balance — where to draw lines to protect the integrity of the corporate culture and brand, and where to leave space so the local office can do what works best there. By inviting dialogue on relevant issues while making a genuine effort to understand the day-to-day realities of the local office, you open up a process that allows them to evolve organically into a natural mix of corporate, regional and office cultures. The goal is not to make every local office culture exactly the *same* as the corporate culture, but to have all offices be in harmony — complementary pieces in one, unified puzzle.

For example, earlier in my career, I spent two years helping a pharmaceutical company open markets in Latin America, which included managing a team of professionals from the Caribbean, Chile, Argentina and Colombia. I received a request from a Chilean male direct report for maternity leave. At the time, this was not as common as it has become in the U.S. and Europe — and it was not part of the corporate culture. However, I knew that in Chile a birth involves many social interactions and formal festivities that traditionally require the presence of both the mother and father. Being sensitive to local customs meant granting the request, but I also had to then manage the team's perceptions and develop a sense of cultural congruence among those who initially felt the situation was unfair.

As you strive to bridge corporate and local office cultures, look for common ground to bring people together and ease differences, including "cultureless" elements like technology, educational experiences, and personal interests such as travel and hobbies. Certain kinds of intellectual capital can also help people connect and understand one another. For example, there are significant cultural differences between a young U.S. woman and a conservative, traditionally raised man from Saudi Arabia, but when you emphasize that they are both engineers, you remind them that they share a common language. Framing team interactions to focus on what people have in common can enhance the sense of collaboration, open doors to other levels of understanding, and help ease many cultural tensions or misunderstandings that occur during daily interactions.

Match Your Management Style to Cultural Orientation

The complexity of today's multicultural workforce makes gender and cultural intelligence, and adaptability, critical attributes for effective leadership. When I teach or consult on leadership issues, I start with the leader's core, authentic self. I believe a leader must explore and understand their inner voice — its strengths as well as its prejudices. Most other leadership skills are built on, or even depend on, one's self-awareness.

Once you've established that foundation, you stand a much better chance of success in the next phase of leadership development: empathy. To lead someone, you have to be able to "get in their shoes" and understand their concerns and motivations.

Both self-awareness and empathy become especially important when managing across cultures. The latter can be challenging in that you may need to empathize with individuals whose values, assumptions and perspectives are very foreign to you. You will need to learn new things and stretch your imagination to "get" these individuals in a meaningful way. This will take you out of your "comfort zone" sometimes, but as you develop the capacity to empathize with those who are different, you will become a more effective manager and increase the value you offer to your organization.

To build your cultural intelligence and give you a better starting framework for managing those from other cultures, it is helpful to go back to the frameworks we covered in Chapter 5. Hofstede's dimensions may be of particular interest since his initial data involved surveys of thousands of IBM employees located in more than 50 countries — a good match if you're tasked with managing a multinational corporation's diverse workforce! Here I will look at a few of the most common cultural orientations that you will face as a manager, and offer some tips on how to adapt management styles and activities to "fit" them.

Individualist Orientation

In this dimension, individuals have a high degree of autonomy and are self-directed. They do not need a group consensus before taking action, and in general they think in terms of the "I" more than the "we."

As a manager, an important step in motivating someone with this orientation is to explain how a project, process or change will benefit them.

You'll also want to give them plenty of opportunities to ask questions, make suggestions, and even raise objections, especially early on.

With a mixed team, remember that those with an individualist orientation will require support and coaching on being empathetic and collaborative. These qualities may not surface without a "push" from you.

For example, let's say you have a team where U.S. employees (high on the individualist scale) work with employees from Japan and Mexico (low on the individualist scale). You would want to coach your U.S. talent to modify expectations regarding decision-making (forming group consensus is important so you can't push for on-the-spot individual decisions), turn-around (schedules and deadlines are less rigid), and even types of words, phrases and tones to use or avoid.

Collectivist Orientation

Group norms and goals are vital for those with a collectivist orientation, which is common throughout Asia, Latin America and the Middle East. Someone from this background looks to peers and on many occasions friends and relatives to contextualize perceptions and shape values. Decisions typically require a certain level of group participation and approval, which often makes the process more time-consuming.

If you're from an individualist culture like the U.S. and will now manage a team with more collectivist members — say, in your company's new location in China — you'll need to reverse some of your usual assumptions and ways of operating. You'll want to explain how a project, process or change is good for the group rather than specific individuals. You should bring the group together for questions, comments and exchange of ideas. Give the group time and space to work together and consult with each other throughout the team-building process. If possible, participate in the "external" dialogue that happens in these cultures with peers and others who are part of the group's expanded contextual reality. The way you manage time, milestones and performance may also need to shift to reflect a more collective mentality rather than just focusing on individuals.

Hierarchical Orientation

People with a hierarchical orientation respect a top-down system of authority and defer power based on criteria such as rank, title, experience, and class. Employees will "know" their place and be reticent to challenge or question those above them. We saw an extreme example of the downside of this dimension when we discussed the case of Korean Air, where co-pilots didn't challenge pilots on errors that turned out to be fatal.

In terms of management, if your normal style tends to be more open-ended and democratic, be aware that this will not be productive with a team that has a hierarchical orientation. Instead, you need to leverage your position, experience and professional prestige and provide strong guidelines and structure about how things should be done. Pay attention to seniority and power dynamics both inside the team and in terms of how the company communicates with the team. If a message is especially important, consider having it come from a senior executive to maximize attention and respect.

Participative Orientation

In the U.S., and many countries in Europe, people tend to feel that everyone has, or should have, access to power. People respect expertise more than position, and are often comfortable challenging those at even the upper levels of authority.

With a team whose members have this orientation, you can be sure there will be more participation and engagement in decision-making processes — which has both benefits and drawbacks. As a manager, you have to find the right balance — providing a forum that invites discussion, questions, and challenges, but also subtly influencing and directing (and sometimes setting limits on the debate) to keep a process on track. Even when a decision or action requires a more hierarchical framework, it is important to explain your point of view and make sure participative team members feel they are being treated as equals.

Control/Certainty Orientation

In some cultures, like Japan, predictability, knowledge of details and control are very important. People coming from these cultures tend to avoid risks and feel uncomfortable with flux — they want black and white, not shades of gray. Ambiguity or lack of control is often equated with the possibility of failure — which can carry severe sanctions and shame. (Suicide is still an accepted response to certain types of failure in some countries.)

When considering team composition, be aware of these characteristics. If you have a project where details are extremely important and there is no room for ambiguity or risk-taking, someone with this orientation is a great fit. But you're inviting problems if you assign that same person to a project that involves much trial and error and will need to evolve quickly.

If you are managing a team or individuals with this orientation, always provide as much information as possible, including clear rules, instructions and attainable benchmarks. Reassurance can be important. At the start of a project, you might provide examples of similar project or team successes. Throughout the process, monitor anxiety, anticipate potential rough spots, and be prepared to step in and demonstrate that everything is still under control and there is a clear path toward a successful outcome.

Creative Orientation

Unlike the previous orientation, some cultures, and individuals within cultures, embrace uncertainty and risk as natural parts of an essentially creative approach. Drawn to improvising, brainstorming, weighing different options, and thinking outside the box, such people are not daunted by failure and do not take it personally. For them, a failure is just something to be understood and examined for insights that will drive the next effort. In some cases, failure may even be praised as a sign of courage, innovation or leadership.

As with all the orientations, this one has pros and cons depending on the type of project. For managers, one key is to engineer processes to focus on continuous learning and improvement and ensure good information flow. Individuals with a creative orientation will thrive in a more open environment without rigid rules; at the same time, it will probably be up to you as the manager to keep people focused and moving toward the stated goals. It may be necessary to remind such individuals that you're "the boss" and that there are important objective criteria, like cost and return on investment, that must be factored in.

Achievement Orientation

"Live to work" is the motto for people with this orientation. They take pride in what they do and define themselves in the context of their profession. In some cases the value they attach to work may even make it a priority over family and friends. They are therefore intense about the outcomes of their work, whether measured by quality, productivity, or efficiency.

U.S. managers, particularly those accustomed to working with male peers, may find this orientation very natural, but should keep in mind that attitudes may still need to shift or be self-regulated when dealing with females, Millennials or foreign nationals who seek more balance in a multiplicity of social roles. Some European countries also have a unique mix — individuals may have an achievement orientation in general, yet be accustomed to longer vacation periods, maternity leaves, and holidays that are common in Europe.

People from this orientation welcome a manager's emphasis on per-formance and results — and want to be rewarded accordingly. Also keep in mind that expectations flow both ways. Achievement-oriented team members have no problem with you communicating a sense of urgency, but they also expect you to be responsive when managerial direction or support is needed. To maintain their respect, you have to deliver what you promise and put forth maximum effort at all times.

Quality-of-Life Orientation

In this orientation, people seek a balance between the professional and personal. They assume that the schedule should have time for family events, friends, vacations and avocational pursuits. They believe each day should combine work, fun and rest, and are comfortable navigating the transitions. They might see those who focus exclusively on work as one-dimensional and lacking a full and meaningful life.

If you're a manager with an achievement orientation, you may struggle with the expectations of quality-of-life team members to some degree. It may help to review the growing body of scientific research that shows that a balance of work and life can boost productivity. For example, a *Harvard Business Review* article by Tony Schwartz titled "The Productivity Paradox" reviews the case of Sony Pictures, which brought in personal "energy management" consultants. The consultants encouraged the com-pany to make two fundamental shifts:

- Don't expect people to always be "on" and operating at full speed. Recognize that human beings perform best when allowed to alternate between periods of intense focus and periods of renewal.

- Instead of seeking ways to "get more out of" employees, look for ways to put more *into* them. Invest in meeting their core needs (physical health, emotional well-being, mental clarity, and spiritual significance) so they will be more energized and engaged at work.

After implementing a program around these goals, the consultants reported impressive results: 84% of participants said they felt better able to meet the demands of their job and more engaged, 88% reported feeling more focused and productive, and 90% said they had more energy to bring to work. In the first two years after launching the program, Sony had its most profitable year and one of its highest revenue years.[76]

In other words, don't assume that "achievement" is the opposite of work-life balance, downtime, and addressing personal needs. In fact, better business performance may *depend* on them. In managing people with a quality-of-life orientation, it is important to open up a dialogue with your team about how to promote a sense of balance, to be sensitive to family life and other concerns outside work, and, at the same time, to maintain productivity, quality and customer service. When introducing work changes, emphasize how they will reduce stress or improve quality of life if appropriate. Be open to negotiations with individual team members, while also stressing the interdependence of the team.

Multicultural Management in Action: A Practical Example

Let's use a hypothetical example to explore how what we've learned about managing a multicultural team might play out in practice. Assume you are a U.S.-based manager who has a new team composed of two U.S. females, one Mexican male, one male and one female from China, and one German male. So the team is half women and represents four different countries — that's pretty well-balanced!

Based on country of origin, we know that U.S. and German team members will probably be achievement-oriented, individualistic, and able to tolerate ambiguity as part of a creative process. The team members from Mexico and China will be more likely to respond to hierarchy, want control and certainty, and also have a quality-of-life orientation. Some individuals will be collaborative, others more self-driven. Relationships, propriety and "saving face" will be key for half the team, while the other half is likely to be comfortable with a less personal paradigm.

There will actually be a long list of differences based on cultural background, gender and individual variations. To get this team off to a strong start, your first step should be to help them acknowledge and understand the differences and see them as strategically valuable. Next you will have to be the "bridge" that helps them come to consensus on how to negotiate the different ways the team members socialize, communicate and share information. Depending on the type and purpose of the team, you may also need to help identify a leader, assist in defining objectives and roles, and so on.

That first step — helping team members see and accept their differences — is critical. In my experience, when this is done well at the start, it quickly opens people up to wanting to learn more about each other. That curiosity and willingness to learn goes a long way toward creating the connections necessary for a cohesive, productive team. Similarly, the manager can guide everyone to understand how and why each will respond differently to certain scenarios, then make it clear that he or she will be available to help work out misunderstandings. A manager who displays a high level of gender and cultural intelligence will reassure all team members.

Another important role for you as a manager is to anticipate potential challenges and be ready to intervene if necessary. In this case, for example, you have a male and a female from China. Although Chinese women are in the midst of a real cultural revolution, many traditional ways of thinking and behaving are still norms in work settings. So, even though the team has a 50-50 gender balance, extra cultural sensitivity toward the Chinese woman may be necessary to assure her full engagement.

In China, women still tend to defer to men as the voice in the room. It is very possible that the Chinese woman on this team might essentially allow the Chinese man to speak for both of them — and that the man might expect this. Since you want 100% participation from everyone, and know that the Chinese woman will have unique ideas that are valuable to the team, you will need to work with both Chinese team members to reframe their assumptions and behavior.

It may help to evoke your corporate culture as a framework for appropriate work styles. You may want to have a session with the Chinese team members to help the woman understand that she can be more outspoken and the man should adopt a more collaborative stance. You could also encourage the U.S. women to support the Chinese woman, coach her in ways to participate and "be heard," and take action if it seems that she is not getting the opportunity to speak her mind. For cultural reasons, the Chinese woman may need to be "invited" to participate until she gets more comfortable.

Thinking about how different cultures see power, you will also want to make sure there is a good dialogue regarding how the team members will manage communications and accountability. Set clear expectations about following rules, modifying rules, and the appropriateness of challenging authority — the latter will be fairly easy for some, but extremely difficult for others.

There are many other differences to explore with this simple team, but I'll save that for the exercises at the end of the section. Here's my best advice for managing *any* differences: Build your cultural intelligence and let empathy be your guide!

CHAPTER 9
Managing in a Flat World:
Virtual Teams Need Real Guidance

Technology is helping companies leverage skills, talent, and expertise around the world at a low cost and in real time. It has transformed the way we work in our home office and with colleagues in other countries forever. Travel is no longer necessary. Data exchange, team meetings, reports, strategy sessions, purchasing — almost everything can now be done via video conference, email, and phone.

Technology has "flattened" the world in terms of removing obstacles to accessibility and connection. But the "flat world" also presents new challenges. When you're not face to face with someone, it is easier than ever to simply assume "your way" of conducting business, communicating and setting expectations. But "flat" does not mean "cultureless" — and if we fail to build cultural awareness and sensitivity into "flat" interactions, conflicts and misunderstandings will be common and performance will suffer.

With a gender-balanced, multicultural team, managing in a flat world can be quite demanding — you have to facilitate understanding, be empathetic, and bridge gaps without the benefit of people being able to see and "read" each other in person! There are also new factors to consider. For example, when creating a virtual team, you have to think about how the anonymity and invisibility that technology provides could impact individual team members and interactions. Again and again, clients tell me that although technology has accelerated the exchange of information for their teams, it has also led to more miscommunication and lost time.

I've been witnessing a good example of this during an ongoing coaching engagement I have with a senior executive woman at a large, global company. She is part of a three-tier multicultural team with subgroups from the U.S., Japan and the U.K. They exchanged information via virtual means for more than 10 months with very limited success. In fact, although the team leader, a European male, had clearly tried to be diplomatic and accommodating, various team members felt frustrated that they were unheard, others were confused about the team's direction, and still others apparently felt offended.

Top management in this case failed to recognize the complexities of cross-cultural interactions. They assumed everything could be handled virtually and did little to promote a dialogue about what was holding up the project. As a result, valuable time was wasted, individual morale was damaged, and a key project derailed. Finally, the leaders decided to invest the time and money to get everyone to a set of face-to-face meetings. The first day was spent with a consulting group who helped unravel the issues and feelings that had been keeping the group at a standstill. Having done that work, and now able to communicate face to face, the rest of the week was very productive and set the team back on course to achieve their target.

No manager should assume that competency, intellect, shared business goals and the power of modern technology will be enough to overcome cultural differences. Similarly, human needs should not be overlooked just because you are operating in a virtual environment. In fact, such environments make it even more important for managers to provide clear guidelines, intervene to avert or resolve conflicts, and provide encouragement and praise. To focus only on business goals and leave technological interactions essentially "unmanaged" is to invite psychological and motivational stagnation, unnecessary conflicts and misunderstandings, and underperformance.

With all that said, it's undeniable that virtual teams are becoming the norm for many organizations, so let's explore some tips to help you get the benefits without suffering the pitfalls.

Education, Training — and Bridge Building

Educating your team about cultural differences — and similarities — is a critical first step toward creating a more cohesive, integrated team and work environment. With virtual teams, this is even more important because there is a higher risk of individuals failing to *see* (literally) the differences in other team members. Operating on the same technological platform does not make team members the "same" — nor does it magically ensure equal participation and treatment. Detached from immediate, in-person repercussions, it can also become all too easy to forget the impact (positive or adverse) that our words or responses can have on others.

So, if your team is dispersed across multiple countries, and your travel budget is limited, how can you educate your team and set the right tone for good performance? Keep in mind that traditional training isn't the only option — in fact, it's just one of five approaches that I will discuss in this section. Just as importantly, remember that the goal here is not just to disseminate information but to build connections between team members. How best to do that will vary depending on the team members, your corporate culture, and other circumstances — but these five techniques will give you a starting point.

Bridge-Building Approach 1: Profile Sharing

One simple technique I use to help team members educate each other is to have each person prepare a brief personal profile. I generally give them prompts so they are all providing similar information. For example:

- List your hobbies and special interests. What are you most passionate about?
- Describe the members of your family.
- Tell a story about a moment when you felt a high degree of success or accomplishment.
- Tell a story about a situation that was challenging or difficult and how you handled the obstacles.
- Describe something humorous about you that happened in the past year.
- Describe your country of origin — be sure to mention a few things that usually only natives know about it.
- Share a few pictures of your country or family and explain how they are meaningful to you.

I usually ask that this exchange occur weeks before a team assembles, in the forming phase, while goals and expectations are still being developed. This gets team-building off to a good, personally connective start. It has value for multicultural and homogeneous teams alike and sets a positive tone for other phases of team building and interpersonal communications.

It is almost always easier to communicate and collaborate when we know something meaningful about the other person.

Bridge-Building Approach 2: Research the Other

Another good technique, particularly with data-driven professionals who may not be comfortable talking about themselves, is to ask team members to *research* the country or countries of fellow team members. Ask them to find maps, summarize history, report on current events from the nation's business newspapers, and put together a file of textual and visual information to help someone become an "instant expert" on the culture and country they're researching.

Typically I then have team members share the results of their research with each other, and also suggest that everyone prepare a list of questions that pop up as they review the data. This gives people a secure, sanctioned and scientific-feeling way to explore differences, deepen understandings, and show their interest in learning about each other. Because of the format, there is less risk and fear of offending someone or falling into a "culturally incorrect" scenario.

Participants almost always have fun with this approach. It creates a quick, solid body of shared knowledge about individual team members while providing insights about how the team will work best together. Again, this option is particularly useful when you have members who are more private, have difficulty socializing, prefer to communicate with "hard data" rather than emotions, or have a contextual boundary between their professional and personal lives.

Bridge-Building Approach 3:
Unify Around the Corporate Mission/Vision

Your corporate mission/vision, core values, code of ethics and similar materials provide excellent "common ground" for diverse team members to explore. Your HR team may be able to provide resources for this exercise, or you can develop a brief survey with the input of the team. Either way the goal is to have team members share their interpretations and feelings regarding the corporate culture. With a multicultural team in particular, you might also ask them to talk about any differences between the corporate culture and their local office culture.

As part of the discussion, highlight the similarities and differences among team members. In my experience, people are usually pleasantly surprised to see how much they have in common. Areas that do not overlap then become points for sincere discussion that can provide valuable insight on personal or cultural differences that go beyond corporate culture.

This approach is especially valuable with multicultural teams where members haven't worked together before. It's a good way for everyone to see how each member thinks and applies their values, simultaneously spotlighting individual contributions while stimulating a sense of being connected by central concepts. Ideally, at the end of this exercise, team members have begun to discover a unifying voice and common points of reference that will serve everyone well throughout the team's work.

An added benefit of this exercise for you as a manager is that it offers a good snapshot of how aligned team members' values and practices are with the corporate culture and protocols, as well as how team members interact in a business-based discussion. This gives you a chance to spot and address any areas that may need attention.

Bridge-Building Approach 4: Let the Experts Do It

Bringing in experts to help with training and bridge-building has many advantages: focused expertise, dedicated professionals who don't have to juggle other tasks, and the value of an outside perspective. This approach is especially appropriate if the company has a very traditional corporate culture that hasn't changed much over the decades, but now needs to evolve due to growth in global markets.

In fact, it's a good reality check for senior executives and managers to look around the company and ask, who has knowledge and expertise of multicultural environments here? If you don't have an answer, it's better to bring in an outside expert than to risk something going wrong.

The type of engagement will vary depending on needs, but I often recommend a short two-day session as a good, quick way to facilitate dialogue about differences, set a respectful tone, and light up good communication paths for a team. I should emphasize that, especially with multicultural challenges, it is important to work with someone who has experience with the cultures involved and is current with best practices. Outdated training can sometimes create as many problems as it solves.

It can also be worthwhile to have an outside expert help assess your current efforts. On numerous occasions, multinational companies have asked me to develop training related to diversity, and issues like harassment, and I have been quite surprised to see the existing training tools they offered. Too often I find an "old school" approach that relies on tabulating a certain number of hours rather than substantive training meant to transform perceptions and behaviors.

Bridge-Building Approach 5: Make the Connection in Person

With virtual teams especially, I strongly recommend that the initial kick-off involve a face-to-face meeting in a real-world setting. There is just no substitute for personal, one-on-one contact, especially when trying to establish congruence with international teams. Bringing the team together to truly see and hear each other before they begin working is a good investment that will pay off in clearer, more respectful communications when the team goes "virtual."

In many office environments, the reliance on technology ends up depriving professionals of the social benefits of human interaction. Various studies have shown the power of social networks, including, as we cited earlier, increased production of oxytocin and other beneficial physiological impacts. "Social media" isn't always the best way to get that networking started with a team.

A professor of mine once told us about teleconferencing with a colleague in Russia. They both agreed that technology had given them a quick and affordable way to exchange ideas — but also that they greatly missed the feeling of sitting in their favorite restaurant together and sharing a good shot of vodka at the end of a workday. That's a valuable lesson — some types of bridge-building just can't be done online!

Ensuring Clear Communications

There's no way around it — virtual communication modes amplify the risk of misunderstanding, confusion, personal conflict, errors and other problems that can undermine performance. That makes it all the more important when managing a virtual team to do everything you can to offset those risks. There are two major areas that merit attention: strategically structuring virtual communications, and making sure team members have good online etiquette.

In terms of structure, keep in mind that "virtual" now gives you many different options: video conferencing, webinars, teleconferences, email, webcast, collaborative software, and so on. Don't let communications "just happen," take the time to think about and formally spell out which tools will be most effective for specific purposes. A good first step is to assess team members and get feedback on related issues. For example:

- Are all team members proficient in the technology that you want to use?
- Is there the same degree of connectivity and infrastructure in all the sites/countries?
- Are time zones a factor? If so, how can you structure communications to be accommodating and equitable for all? For example, avoid putting people in a position where they have to do a videoconference at a local time when they would be in bed!
- Consider creating guidelines to identify what technology and communication modes are best for different purposes.

Similarly, be strategic about what communication modes will work best for specific team members. Consider who needs "face time," who prefers collaboration and who works well with minimal feedback. If you have a majority of women, you might encourage them to use tools that support their ability to befriend and create social networks, such as teleconferencing.

As manager, you may have to strike a balance between team member communication preferences and what will work best for project objectives. With a virtual, global team, particularly if it includes professionals who are not naturally social, there may be a tendency to choose the path of least resistance and exchange information mostly through email or voicemail. But that is not always the most effective or efficient communication path. Sometimes the direct, real-time interaction of a videoconference or collaborative web application is the best way forward.

Managing communications in a virtual setting is challenging. Mistakes are easier to make and often more time-consuming to repair. At one of my client companies, an HR person recently explained that she was working overtime due to an "email blast" sent by the legal department related to early retirement. Because the email was not carefully worded, it gave many people the impression that he/she was expected to begin coordinating early retirement as part of phasing out their current job. This was not intended, but it created uncertainty and fear for many employees and a major distraction from their work. The corrective communication that followed couldn't totally erase that impact. It's a good lesson to reinforce for team members — exercise extra caution with communications through email. Once you hit "send" it's out there forever.

Online Etiquette: New Challenges in Virtual Interactions

In personal interactions, most professionals have a well-developed sense of etiquette. There are appropriate and inappropriate ways to say things or present oneself. The same is true online, but since the medium is relatively new, the rules are still evolving and not always well known, especially among older managers and employees. Unfortunately, it often takes a series of costly miscommunications and conflicts to convince companies that they should start training employees in online etiquette.

The ease with which we can send and receive online messages makes it easy to overlook how much they communicate (and potentially miscommunicate) about you and your organization. It's not just the words or attached content — fonts, formats, signatures, colors and other elements are all part of the presentation. Potential problems with misinterpretation, inconsistency, interpersonal conflict, and undermining the corporate brand, can begin to outweigh the convenience. If you have a team that is trying to balance gender and multicultural differences and using *only* virtual communication, the likelihood of negative outcomes rises exponentially.

Whole books and training courses are available on this topic if you want to cover it in detail. But to start, here are some basic points for you and your team to consider along with some simple actions that will help you avoid online faux pas:

- Who should have access to email? Discuss privacy issues and remind people to be careful not to "accidentally" transmit sensitive or private information. For example, often someone hits "Forward" to pass on a piece of information to a new recipient. However, "Forward" typically includes the entire chain of emails with the original sender — if these are not erased, the new recipient may see comments that were not intended for them.

- Encourage everyone to think carefully about information flow and not clutter up everyone's "in box" by cc-ing all team members with messages that only need to be seen by one or two people. At the same time, provide guidance on when it *is* appropriate to cc everyone to keep all team members in the loop on important developments.
- Discuss appropriate protocols regarding title, use of first or last name, and openings or closings that may be important across the cultures of different team members.
- Develop guidelines for when to communicate via online vehicles and when it is better to pick up the phone, schedule a videoconference, or, if possible, convey something in person. Also clarify lines of authority that relate to communications — who determines who needs to know what?
- Assure transparency and improve team buy-in by formalizing online communication guidelines, distributing to all team members and requesting feedback before finalizing.
- Warn team members to be extremely cautious about using humor and slang that may not be understood by others, and to steer clear of "hot button" topics like religion, politics, and social views. Particularly with a diverse team, remind everyone that comments they consider harmless may still be offensive, disrespectful or imposing to others.
- Tap other internal and external resources for more guidance. Your HR department may already have a Do/Don't list for online communications, and there are numerous resources on the web that you can use or modify for your team's purposes.

Creating "Virtual" Trust and Collaboration

Throughout this book we've discussed the importance of trust in building a high-performing team. Trust is the number one attribute people seek from a leader, and the foundation for effective collaboration. It is paramount to developing individual engagement and commitment.

Developing trust has a central role in the training and coaching I do. In my experience, when developed and managed properly, few qualities have a more powerful impact in helping individuals and teams reach their full potential. With a diverse team, trust is vital both for inspiring "follow-ership" and helping individual team members get through challenges that may arise due to their differences.

Creating trust is even more important if your diverse team is virtual — but the virtual setting also makes it more elusive. I have found that one good way to build trust — in any setting — is to address the topic directly with your team. For example, consider these team exercises:

- Ask team members to define trust, then share and discuss the different definitions.
- Have team members discuss the consequences of distrust. Ask if they have examples where a lack of trust derailed a process or undermined performance.
- Identify possible obstacles to building trust that the team faces? (Gender and cultural differences, geography, economic pressures, etc.)
- Ask the team to come up with possible solutions to the trust challenges that are identified. If possible, form consensus around executing a set of trust solutions.
- Discuss the impact of trust on collaboration. Review the kinds of collaboration that the team will engage in and explore the specific types of trust that will be important for success.
- Have the team create lists of desirable behaviors that enhance trust and collaboration, and undesirable behaviors that deter trust and collaboration. Emphasize the need to be aware of what's on these lists in daily interactions.

During the forming stage, these exercises open up a trust dialogue for team members, while also giving you as a manager a chance to identify areas of potential risk. They are also good exercises to return to if the team seems to be struggling at another point in its lifecycle. I have often found that trust issues are an underlying cause of problems that a team is experiencing and that surfacing these issues is the first step to getting the team back on track.

Exploring trust can also provide insights on related issues. For example, I once did a week-long leadership training program for high-performing female professionals in mid-level positions. They came from the U.S., China, Japan, Israel, Egypt, Germany, and a range of other cultures. During an exercise on developing trust, I had each woman describe her relationship with her boss and how "free" she felt to execute the trust-building concepts we had discussed. My goal was to elicit a conversation that would help all participants understand the obstacles some women face in taking the initiative to develop trust.

Sure enough, there were many "aha!" moments as we went around the room and women shared the cultural realities of their country and local office culture. What became clear was that it was not reasonable for corporate headquarters to ignore the challenges these women faced from social and cultural contexts. They would need to provide additional support and intervention to help these talented women achieve their professional goals and realize their full potential as leaders.

A Concluding Thought: You Can't Ask What You Can't Do!

I want to close this section on team building — and the book — with a little pep talk just for you. As I've said throughout the book, managers have a central, decisive role in their organization's ability to leverage gender and cultural differences for better business performance. You are ultimately the one who sets the tone and provides the most visible model for trust, respect, inclusiveness, and other important qualities that ensure successful collaboration. Indeed, this is true not only for the teams you manage, but also for peers and stakeholders throughout the organization.

To become all you can in this role, you must first be honest about where you are. There is no shame in acknowledging limitations — that's the first step to growing beyond them! So always give yourself the time and space for self-reflection on the issues you will face with a diverse team, including your most basic feelings about cultural differences, exploring new ideas, and change.

In general, I find that when assessing themselves on challenges related to gender and cultural diversity, managers fall into one of three categories:

- I embrace the complexity — it's a great learning experience!
- I'm ok with some things related to diversity, but unclear or unsure about others
- I'm uncomfortable and feel trapped or frustrated

These are not static — no matter where you are, the goal should be to challenge yourself to improve. But an initial gauging of your skill and comfort in navigating diverse environments and cultures gives you a clearer idea of your challenges — and of what support you may need.

No one should feel bad about asking for help when it comes to understanding gender and cultural differences — this is a vast, complicated subject! Some organizations have good internal programs to help you in this area, and all can contract expert consultants who specialize in this field and have developed proven training and coaching programs to help you move quickly from initial discomfort or confusion toward the gender and cultural intelligence that will make you a more effective leader.

I wrote *Can You Afford to Ignore Me?* as a way to give you some direction on this important journey. While it is meant to be a thorough guide that you can return to again and again, I also hope you will use it as a launching pad for further exploration. If you found a quote or statistic particularly intriguing or valuable, use the references section at the end of the book to locate the source, then go read the full article or book. If you really want to accelerate the learning process, consider pursuing training or one-on-one coaching. Who knows — maybe we will even work together sometime soon!

Ignoring differences, and team members with differences, is simply not an option given today's workforce. And gender and cultural awareness and sensitivity is not something you can "fake." It's time to begin appreciating authentic differences — your own and those of others. It's time to transform the "ignored" into the "inspired"!

SECTION IV
Reflections, Exercises, Tips and Takeaways

Reflections:

- This section, by its nature, included many exercises and tips. Take a moment to revisit some you found particularly valuable. How can you modify and use them for the team or teams you currently manage?
- How knowledgeable are you about your corporate culture? Do the values and practices of the corporate culture align with your own? How does the corporate culture impact your team? Do you have team members that may be struggling to resolve differences between the corporate culture and their local office culture?
- Reflect on your comfort level and curiosity when it comes to learning about and interacting with other cultures. Rate yourself on a scale of 1 to 10, where 1 is Very Uncomfortable and 10 is Very Comfortable. Now think about what you can do to move yourself up the scale!
- If your company has diversity programs, think about whether outcomes have been positive, negligible or negative. Based on what you've learned in this section, and in the book, where can you see room for improvement?

Exercises:

- As a team, explore the concept of assimilation. If you are a multinational company, ask team members if they've felt pressured to conform to the company's "home culture." Talk about the difference between alignment and assimilation and identify examples of both.

- Check your perceptions of your team against theirs. Start by having everyone write down how the team does (or will do) its work on a day-to-day basis. List team strengths and weaknesses. Identify the team's central objective or value, as well as the obstacles to realizing its potential. Then meet as a group to share what everyone has written and, if necessary, align perceptions. If your team has a long enough life span, consider repeating this exercise during the forming stage, again after the team has had time to work together, and then later when the team has a fairly stable identity or has reached the end of its lifecycle.
- Revisit our hypothetical example at the end of Chapter 8. How many other challenges can you anticipate based on analyzing this team's gender and cultural composition?
- Check with your HR department or look online to find and take tests related to stereotyping and prejudices.

Tips:

- *Travel.* There is no substitute for experience. The more you expose yourself to cultural differences, the more comfortable you will be about managing them in the workplace. If you don't have the time or budget to travel literally, use online resources to do "virtual" globetrotting.
- *Stay informed.* It is easy to become "cocooned," getting all our news and information from just a few familiar sources that represent similar perspectives. With a diverse workforce and a global economy, that "cocoon" is a major disadvantage. Challenge yourself to read/watch a range of business media — not just mainstream papers like the *Wall Street Journal* and *Financial Times,* but also publications cited in this book such as *Harvard Business Review* and *McKinsey Quarterly.* About to engage with a multicultural team or welcome a new foreign national to your team? Read publications from *their* country to gain perspective and provide a great "connector" for your first meeting.

- *Try this at home!* During my work with a group of multinational companies in Brazil, the CFO of one company approached me after I had presented some key points on gender and said, "What you have explained about gender is not only significant for me at work, but also as a father of two girls. This discussion has opened my eyes to being sure I understand what messages I give them. Thank you." This is an excellent point — being more aware of gender and culture differences can enrich our personal lives and communities as well as our work environments!

Takeaways:

1. Teams benefit from diversity. Numerous studies have shown that teams with better gender and cultural balance outperform homogeneous teams. Managers in the global economy must leverage the unique skills, talents, experiences, and outlooks of a diverse workforce to remain competitive and achieve optimal results.

2. After defining a team's type and purpose, it is beneficial to look at the available talent pool from the perspective of gender and culture. What you've learned in this book, including Hofstede's cultural dimensions, will help you compose a balanced team with complementary behavioral tendencies as well as complementary skills. That balance can go a long way in simplifying management, enabling team members to perform to their full potential, and ensuring that the project will achieve its objectives.

3. Communication structure is essential. Investing time to set up and explain communication protocols for a project will pay off in less misunderstandings, greater efficiency, and better performance.

4. With multinational teams, it is critical to travel to the market of each member and make sure you understand local norms. If other senior managers have managed in the markets you are responsible for, ask them for guidance.

5. When dealing with virtual teams, advocate for an initial face-to-face meeting whenever possible. Technology offers many tools to allow team members in different locations to communicate,

but it is not the best "venue" to help individuals understand each other and develop group cohesion and congruence. Virtual teams can easily derail if technology and business goals are the only things that connect them.

ACKNOWLEDGEMENTS

Writing a book is a work of love, dedication and will. I have been surrounded by people with these attributes who not only appreciate my work, but also care for me. I want to acknowledge their efforts, goodwill and love.

First and foremost, my husband Daniel Dennehy, who I call DJ, is a brilliant, passionate, dedicated man whose support through the last four years has been unconditional. Many times, that support was the force that pushed me forward.

My children, Aisha Marie and Daniel Jose, are also a vital internal force, inspiring my desire to create a piece of work that will make them feel proud and empowered. I hope this book shows them that they can achieve what may seem impossible or out of reach if they strive with passion and unequivocal purpose.

I am grateful to Joanne Pompeo, who is not only an incredibly smart and competent professional, but also the most caring and committed friend I could wish for to share this journey.

My siblings, Fernando, Ana and Federico Rodriguez, held me many times during this process and kept me going, reminding me of our heritage and our inner strength.

So many friends and students helped me throughout this process — I wish there were space to list you all by name. I do want to call out Angela Arrington for her support when I first began thinking about this project, and Jean Zamzow, who spent hours discussing the book and giving me ideas on how to frame the concepts with clarity. To all my students who cheered me on and kept asking "When will the book be ready?" — thank you, and here it is!

A special acknowledgement goes to Hank Walshak, who dedicated many afternoons to supporting me and helping me craft the first draft of the book.

Don Bertschman picked up the baton for the critical lap that got us across the finish line successfully. As an editor, his listening, imagination and extraordinary care for quality have been instrumental in giving this book its final shape and style.

This book evolved out of my work, and is deeply tied to my ongoing consulting and coaching, so I also want to thank my clients, the wonderful corporate professionals who have entrusted me to help navigate the sometimes bumpy roads to leadership, individual and team performance. Thank you to the fabulous professional women I've coached from the U.S., Latin America, the Czech Republic, and Asia — may your journey continue to be bright and full of success. And to the executives, male and female, who have brought me in to work in their organizations — thank you for your trust and your vision.

As I conclude my own journey (at least for this book!) I want to recognize one more person. Stephanie McMahon, a student of mine at Duquesne University, was smart, brilliant, feisty, loud and full of life. Unfortunately, we lost her too soon. When I last saw her she could barely talk, but the one thing she managed to say was, "the book." Stephanie, wherever you are, this is for you, in memory of your love for life and fantastic spirit. I miss you.

REFERENCES

[1] Dezso, Cristian L. and Ross, David Gaddis. "Does Female Representation in Top Management Improve Firm Performance? A Panel Data Investigation." Robert H. Smith School Research Paper No. RHS 06-104, March 9, 2011.

[2] Steinem, Gloria. "'Women's Liberation' Aims to Free Men, Too." *The Washington Post*, June 7, 1970.

[3] "Women's History in America." Women's International Center. Published online at www.wic.org/misc/history.htm.

[4] U.S. Department of Education, National Center for Education Statistics.

[5] "Education Counts: Benchmarking Progress in 19 WEI Countries." UNESCO Institute for Statistics. September 2007.

[6] As seen on *The Charlie Rose Show*, November 7, 2011.

[7] U.S. Census Bureau. *Historical Income Tables.* Available online at www.census.gov/hhes/www/income/data/historical/people/index.html.

[8] "The Gender Wage Gap: 2011." Fact Sheet from the Institute for Women's Policy Research available online at www.iwpr.org.

[9] "Women's Earnings and Income." Catalyst. August 2012. Available online at www.catalyst.org/publication/217/womens-earnings-and-income.

[10] Flom, Barbara M. and Stephanie A. Scharf. "Report of the Sixth Annual National Survey on Retention and Promotion of Women in Law Firms." The NAWL Foundation and the National Association of Women Lawyers. October 2011.

[11] "Women's Earnings and Income." Catalyst. August 2012. Available online at www.catalyst.org/publication/217/womens-earnings-and-income.

[12] *The World's Women 2010.* U.N. Department of Economic and Social Affairs. New York: 2010.

[13] *Women and the Economy.* Report by the U.S. Congress Joint Economic Committee, August 2010.

[14] *The World's Women 2010.* U.N. Department of Economic and Social Affairs. New York: 2010.

[15] Hartmann, Susan. *The Home Front and Beyond: American Women in the 1940s.* Macmillan Publishing Company: 1983.

[16] "11 Tips on Getting More Efficiency Out of Women." *Mass Transportation Magazine*, July 1943.

[17] *Rosie the Riveter: Women Working During World War II.* National Park Service online exhibit at www.nps.gov/pwro/collection/website/delana.htm.

[18] *Rosie the Riveter: Women Working During World War II.* National Park Service online exhibit at www.nps.gov/pwro/collection/website/rosie.htm.

[19] Hong, Lu and Scott E. Page. "Groups of Diverse Problem Solvers Can Outperform Groups of High-Ability Problem Solvers." *Proceedings of the National Academy of Sciences, Vol. 101, No. 46.* November 16, 2004.

[20] "Diverse Backgrounds and Personalities Can Strengthen Groups." Stanford Graduate School of Business, August 1, 2006.

[21] Toossi, Mitra. "A New Look at Long-Term Labor Force Projections to 2050." *Monthly Labor Review,* November 2006.

[22] Kristof, Nicholas D. "Mistresses of the Universe." *The New York Times,* February 7, 2009.

[23] Ferrary, Michel. "Why Women Managers Shine in a Downturn." *Financial Times,* March 2, 2009.

[24] "Groundbreakers: Using the Strength of Women to Rebuild the World Economy." Ernst & Young, 2009.

[25] Ryan, Michelle and Alex Haslam. "The Glass Cliff: Evidence That Women Are Over-Represented in Precarious Leadership Positions." *British Journal of Management, 16,* June 2005.

[26] Ryan, Michelle and Alex Haslam. "The Road to the Glass Cliff: Differences in the Perceived Suitability of Men and Women for Leadership Positions in Succeeding and Failing Organizations." *The Leadership Quarterly, 19,* 2008.

[27] Sayre, Kate and Michael J. Silverstein. "The Female Economy." *Harvard Business Review,* September 2009.

[28] Cunningham, Jane and Philippa Roberts. *Inside Her Pretty Little Head.* Cyan Books Marshall Cavendish, England: 2006.

[29] "Women Matter: Gender Diversity, a Corporate Performance Driver." *McKinsey Quarterly,* October 2007.

[30] "The Bottom Line: Corporate Performance and Women's Representation on Boards." Catalyst, October 2007.

[31] Daly, Kevin. "Gender Inequality, Growth and Global Aging." Global Economics Paper No. 154. The Goldman Sachs Group, Inc., 2007.

[32] Hudson, Valerie. "Good Riddance: Why Macho Had to Go." *Foreign Policy,* July/August 2009.

[33] Hayes, Jeff. "Women's Median Earnings as a Percent of Men's Median Earnings, 1960-2009." Institute for Women's Policy Research, March 2011.

[34] Carter, Nancy M. and Christine Silva. "Pipeline's Broken Promise." Catalyst, 2010.

[35] Brizendine, Louann. *The Female Brain.* Broadway Books: 2006.

[36] Brizendine, Louann. *The Female Brain.* Broadway Books: 2006.

[37] Gurian, Michael. *Leadership and the Sexes: Using Gender Science to Create Success in Business*. Jossey-Bass/John Wiley: 2008.

[38] Brizendine, Louann. *The Male Brain*. Broadway Books: 2010.

[39] Coates, John M. and Joe Herbert. "Endogenous Steroids and Financial Risk Taking on a London Trading Floor." *Proceedings of the National Academy of Sciences of the U.S.A., Volume 105*, April 22, 2008.

[40] Coates, John. *The Hour Between the Dog and Wolf: Risk Taking, Gut Feelings, and the Biology of Boom and Bust*. The Penguin Press: 2012.

[41] Flanagan, Caitlin. *Girl Land*. Reagan Arthur Books: 2012.

[42] Fels, Anna. *Necessary Dreams: Ambition in Women's Changing Lives*. Anchor: 2005.

[43] Niederle, Muriel and Lise Vesterlund. "Explaining the Gender Gap in Math Test Scores: The Role of Competition." *Journal of Economic Perspectives, Vol. 24, Num. 2*, Spring 2010.

[44] *Merriam-Webster Online Dictionary*. Online at www.Merriam-Webster.com.

[45] Hall, Edward T. *Beyond Culture*. Anchor Books: 1976.
While the basic framework in this section is drawn from Hall's work, my presentation has also been influenced by numerous other researchers and writers who have put their own spin on "high context" and "low context," as well as my experience using this framework in corporate settings. My intent is to offer details of this framework that managers and professionals I've worked with have found valuable, not to provide a complete or literal overview of Hall's work.

[46] Hofstede, Geert, Gert Jan Hofstede and Michael Minkov. *Cultures and Organizations: Software of the Mind, 3rd Revised Edition*. McGraw-Hill: 2010. © Geert Hofstede B.V. Quoted with permission.
While the six dimensions in this section are drawn from the most recent edition of Cultures and Organizations, *my presentation has also been influenced by numerous other researchers and writers who have incorporated Hofstede's work over the past three decades, as well as my experience using the dimensions in corporate settings. My intent is to offer details of the dimensions that managers and professionals I've worked with have found valuable, not to provide a complete or literal overview of Hofstede's work.*

[47] Barta, Thomas, Markus Kleiner and Tilo Neumann. "Is There a Payoff from Top-Team Diversity?" *McKinsey Quarterly*, April 2012.

[48] *The American Heritage® Dictionary of the English Language, 4th Ed*. Houghton Mifflin Company: 2009.

[49] *Merriam-Webster Online Dictionary*. Online at www.Merriam-Webster.com.

[50] Heim, Pat. *In the Company of Women: Turning Workplace Conflict into Powerful Alliances*. Tarcher: 2001.

[51] Sandberg, Sheryl. Quoted from "Women as the Way Forward," a panel discussion at the World Economic Forum's Annual Conference at Davos, Switzerland, January 27, 2012.

[52] Eagly, Alice H. and Linda L. Carli. *Through the Labyrinth: The Truth About How Women Become Leaders*. Harvard Business School Press: 2007.

[53] Frankel, Lois P. *Nice Girls Don't Get the Corner Office: 101 Unconscious Mistakes Women Make That Sabotage Their Careers*. Business Plus: 2004.

[54] Jespersen, Otto. *Growth and Structure of the English Language*. University of Chicago Press: 1982.

[55] Klofstad, Casey A., Rindy C. Anderson and Susan Peters. "Sounds Like a Winner: Voice Pitch Influences Perception of Leadership Capacity in Both Men and Women." *Proceedings of The Royal Society B: Biological Sciences*, July 7, 2012.

[56] "The Warning." Written and directed by Michael Kirk. *PBS Frontline*, first aired October 2009. ©2009 WGBH Educational Foundation. Available online at www.pbs.org/wgbh/pages/frontline/warning/.

[57] Newman, Melanie. "At the Top, Women Still Can't Get a Break from Stereotypes." *Times Higher Education*, March 13, 2008.

[58] Heim, Pat, Susan Murphy and Susan K. Golant. *In the Company of Women*. Tarcher: 2003.

[59] Wojtas, Olga. " 'Strategic' Networking Is the Key to Women's Advancement." *Times Higher Education*, July 4, 2003.

[60] "Women in Leadership: A European Business Imperative." A report by Catalyst and The Conference Board, 2002.

[61] Hewlett, Sylvia. "A Final Push Can Break the Glass Ceiling." *Financial Times*, November 16, 2010.

[62] Desvaus, Georges, Sandrine Devillard-Hoellinger and Mary C. Meaney. "A Business Case for Women." *The McKinsey Quarterly*, September 2008.

[63] Fels, Anna. *Necessary Dreams: Ambition in Women's Changing Lives*. Anchor: 2005.

[64] Babcock, Linda and Sara Laschever. *Women Don't Ask: Negotiation and the Gender Divide*. Princeton University Press: 2003.

[65] Collins, Anna T. "Falling Off the Ladder: Do Women 'Shoot Themselves in the Foot'?" *The Glass Hammer*, January 2009.

[66] Tannen, Deborah. *Talking from 9 to 5: Women and Men at Work*. Harper-Collins: 1994.

[67] Brandon, Rick and Marty Seldman. *Survival of the Savvy: High-Integrity Political Tactics for Career and Company Success*. Simon & Schuster, Inc.: 2004.

[68] Thomas, David A. and Ayesha Kanji. "IBM's Diversity Strategy: Bridging the Workplace and the Marketplace." Harvard Business School Publishing: 2004.

[69] Collins, Jim. *How the Mighty Fall and Why Some Companies Never Give In*. Collins Business Essentials: 2009.

[70] Kotter, John P. *Leading Change*. Harvard Business Review Press: 1996.

[71] Penenberg, Adam L. "Social Networking Affects Brains Like Falling in Love." *Fast Company*, July 1, 2010.

[72] Elfenbein, Hillary Anger and Jeffrey T. Polzer. "Identity Issues in Teams." Harvard Business Publishing, February 2003.

[73] Schrank, Robert. "Two Women, Three Men on a Raft." *Reach for the Top: Women and the Changing Facts of Work Life*. Ed. Nancy A. Nichols. Harvard Business School Press: 1994.

[74] Gratton, Lynda, Elisabeth Kelan, Andreas Voigt, Lamia Walker and Hans-Joachim Wolfram. "Innovative Potential: Men and Women in Teams." The Lehman Brothers Centre for Women in Business at the London Business School: 2007.

[75] As reported online in "Gender-Related Material in the New Core Curriculum." Stanford Graduate School of Business, 2007.

[76] Schwartz, Tony. "The Productivity Paradox: How Sony Pictures Gets More Out of People by Demanding Less." *Harvard Business Review*, June 2010.

ABOUT THE AUTHOR

Elisabet Rodriguez Dennehy is the founder and president of Rodriguez & Associates, a strategic consulting firm headquartered in Pittsburgh, Pennsylvania. The firm specializes in customized leadership development programs for women and related consulting services to help organizations manage and develop female talent.

Elisabet's ground-breaking approach and personal involvement have led to highly effective executive leadership programs for GSK, Westinghouse, UniCredit, Microsoft, the British Chamber of Commerce, the U.S. Business School of Prague, and many other clients throughout the U.S., Latin America, and the European Union. She has also conducted Coaching and Mentoring programs for the University of Pittsburgh in Sao Paulo, Brazil for global companies like Dow, Motorola, PWC and Caterpillar, in Prague for Deloitte, PPG and ABB, and for many companies based in the Pittsburgh region.

In addition to her consulting work, Elisabet serves as lead faculty at the Duquesne University Women's Executive Leadership Program, where she teaches Leadership; Global Issues in Organizations; Ethics; and Change: The Organization as a System.

For more information, visit erodriguezandassociates.com/home.html or email info@erodriguezandassociates.com.